LAW, CRIME AND LAW ENFORCEMENT

EXTRATERRITORIAL APPLICATION OF U. S. CRIMINAL LAW

POLICIES AND PROPOSALS

Law, Crime and Law Enforcement

Additional books in this series can be found on Nova's website under the Series tab.

Additional E-books in this series can be found on Nova's website under the E-book tab.

Laws and Programs

Additional books in this series can be found on Nova's website under the Series tab.

Additional E-books in this series can be found on Nova's website under the E-book tab.

LAW, CRIME AND LAW ENFORCEMENT

EXTRATERRITORIAL APPLICATION OF U. S. CRIMINAL LAW

POLICIES AND PROPOSALS

DARLA A. GARCIA
AND
GRANT T. COLEMAN
EDITORS

Nova Science Publishers, Inc.
New York

For permission to use material from this book please contact us:
Telephone 631-231-7269; Fax 631-231-8175
Web Site: http://www.novapublishers.com

Library of Congress Cataloging-in-Publication Data

ISBN: 978-1-62081-445-1

Published by Nova Science Publishers, Inc. † New York

CONTENTS

PREFACE

Criminal law is usually territorial. It is a matter of the law of the place where it occurs. Nevertheless, a number of American criminal laws apply outside of the United States. Application is generally a question of legislative intent, expressed or implied. In either case, it most often involves crimes committed aboard a ship or airplane, crimes condemned by international treaty, crimes relating to government employees or property overseas, or crimes that have an impact in this country even if planned or committed in part elsewhere. This book discusses the laws and policy surrounding extraterritorial jurisdiction and proposals for furthering accountability.

Chapter 1 - Criminal law is usually territorial. It is a matter of the law of the place where it occurs. Nevertheless, a number of American criminal laws apply outside of the United States. Application is generally a question of legislative intent, expressed or implied. In either case, it most often involves crimes committed aboard a ship or airplane, crimes condemned by international treaty, crimes relating to government employees or property overseas, or crimes that have an impact in this country even if planned or committed in part elsewhere.

Although the crimes over which the United States has extraterritorial jurisdiction may be many, so are the obstacles to their enforcement. For both practical and diplomatic reasons, criminal investigations within another country require the acquiescence, consent, or preferably the assistance, of the authorities of the host country. The United States has mutual legal assistance treaties with several countries designed to formalize such cooperative law enforcement assistance. Searches and interrogations carried out jointly with foreign officials, certainly if they involve Americans, must be conducted within the confines of the Fourth and Fifth Amendments. And the Sixth

Amendment imposes limits upon the use in American criminal trials of depositions taken abroad.

The nation's recently negotiated extradition treaties address some of the features of the nation's earlier agreements which complicate extradition for extraterritorial offenses, that is, dual criminality requirements, reluctance to recognize extraterritorial jurisdiction, and exemptions on the basis of nationality or political offenses. To further facilitate the prosecution of federal crimes with extraterritorial application Congress has enacted special venue, statute of limitations, and evidentiary statutes. To further cooperative efforts, it enacted the Foreign Evidence Request Efficiency Act, P.L. 111-79, which authorizes federal courts to issue search warrants, subpoenas and other orders to facilitate criminal investigations in this country on behalf of foreign law enforcement officials.

Chapter 2 - The United States government uses hundreds of thousands of civilian contractors and employees overseas. They and their dependants are often subject to local prosecution for the crimes they commit abroad. Whether by agreement, practice, or circumstance—sometimes they are not. The Military Extraterritorial Jurisdiction Act (MEJA) permits federal prosecution of certain crimes committed abroad by Defense Department civilian employees, contractors, or their dependants. The Civilian Extraterritorial Jurisdiction Act (CEJA; H.R. 2136) (Representative Price of North Carolina) and S. 1145 (Senator Leahy) would permit federal prosecution for certain crimes committed abroad by the civilian employees, dependants, or contractors of other federal agencies.

The bills would supplement rather than replace MEJA or other provisions of federal extraterritorial jurisdiction. The crimes covered would include various federal violent, corruption, and trafficking offenses. The Attorney General would be responsible to ensure the availability of personnel and other resources necessary for investigation and prosecution of such offenses.

Otherwise applicable statutes of limitation would be suspended during the absence of a suspect from the United States. Prosecutors would be afforded the additional option of trying cases under CEJA in the district in which the employing or contracting agency maintained its headquarters.

Chapter 3 - Statement of Senator Patrick Leahy (D-Vt.), Chairman, Senate Judiciary Committee.

Chapter 4 - Statement of Tara Lee Global Co-Chair, Transnational Litigation DLA Piper LLP (US).

Chapter 5 - Statement by Geoffrey S. Corn Professor of Law, South Texas College of Law, Houston, Texas.

Chapter 6 - Statement of Michael J. Edney Gibson, Dunn & Crutcher LLP.

Chapter 7 - Statement of Lanny A. Breuer, Assistant Attorney General, Criminal Division Department of Justice.

In: Extraterritorial Application … ISBN 978-1-62081-445-1
Editors: D. Garcia and G. Coleman

Chapter 1

EXTRATERRITORIAL APPLICATION OF AMERICAN CRIMINAL LAW*

Charles Doyle

SUMMARY

Criminal law is usually territorial. It is a matter of the law of the place where it occurs. Nevertheless, a number of American criminal laws apply outside of the United States. Application is generally a question of legislative intent, expressed or implied. In either case, it most often involves crimes committed aboard a ship or airplane, crimes condemned by international treaty, crimes relating to government employees or property overseas, or crimes that have an impact in this country even if planned or committed in part elsewhere.

Although the crimes over which the United States has extraterritorial jurisdiction may be many, so are the obstacles to their enforcement. For both practical and diplomatic reasons, criminal investigations within another country require the acquiescence, consent, or preferably the assistance, of the authorities of the host country. The United States has mutual legal assistance treaties with several countries designed to formalize such cooperative law enforcement assistance. Searches and interrogations carried out jointly with foreign officials, certainly if they involve Americans, must be conducted

* This is an edited, reformatted and augmented version of a Congressional Research Service publication, CRS Report for Congress 94-166, dated February 15, 2012.

within the confines of the Fourth and Fifth Amendments. And the Sixth Amendment imposes limits upon the use in American criminal trials of depositions taken abroad.

The nation's recently negotiated extradition treaties address some of the features of the nation's earlier agreements which complicate extradition for extraterritorial offenses, that is, dual criminality requirements, reluctance to recognize extraterritorial jurisdiction, and exemptions on the basis of nationality or political offenses. To further facilitate the prosecution of federal crimes with extraterritorial application Congress has enacted special venue, statute of limitations, and evidentiary statutes. To further cooperative efforts, it enacted the Foreign Evidence Request Efficiency Act, P.L. 111-79, which authorizes federal courts to issue search warrants, subpoenas and other orders to facilitate criminal investigations in this country on behalf of foreign law enforcement officials.

INTRODUCTION

Crime is ordinarily proscribed, tried, and punished according to the laws of the place where it occurs.[1] American criminal law applies beyond the geographical confines of the United States, however, under certain limited circumstances. State prosecution for overseas misconduct is limited almost exclusively to multi-jurisdictional crimes, that is, crimes where some elements of the offense are committed within the state and others are committed beyond its boundaries.[2] A surprising number of federal criminal statutes have extraterritorial application, but prosecutions have been few. This may be because when extraterritorial criminal jurisdiction does exist, practical and legal complications, and sometimes diplomatic considerations, may counsel against its exercise.

CONSTITUTIONAL CONSIDERATIONS

Legislative Powers

The Constitution does not forbid either Congressional or state enactment of laws which apply outside the United States. Nor does it prohibit either the federal government or the states from prosecuting conduct committed abroad.

In fact, several passages suggest that the Constitution contemplates the application of American law beyond the geographical confines of the United States. It speaks, for example, of "felonies committed on the high seas," "offences against the law of nations," "commerce with foreign nations," and of the impact of treaties.[3]

More specifically, it grants Congress the power "[t]o define and punish Piracies and Felonies committed on the high Seas, and Offences against the Law of Nations";[4] the power "[t]o regulate commerce with foreign Nations";[5] and "[t]o make all Laws which shall be necessary and properly for carrying into Execution the foregoing Powers, and all other Powers vested by this Constitution in the Government of the United States, or in any Department or Officer thereof."[6]

The power to define and punish felonies on the high seas and the power under the necessary and proper clause have been referenced in the past as the source of Congress's authority to enacted extraterritorial criminal legislation primarily in a maritime context.[7] The powers have been read broadly to permit overseas application of federal criminal law, even extending to an American vessel at anchor well within the territory of another nation.[8]

Congress's power "[t]o regulate Commerce with foreign Nations,"[9] affords it additional authority in the area. The commerce power, that is, the power "[t]o regulate Commerce with foreign Nations, and among the several States, and with the Indian Tribes," is a power of exceptional breadth domestically.[10] Its reach may be even more extraordinary in an international context,[11] although there is certainly support for a contrary view.[12] In recent cases, the courts have opted for a middle ground. In one, it found that Congress did indeed have the legislative power to proscribe illicit overseas commercial sexual activity by an American who had traveled from the United States to the scene of the crime.[13] Confronted with a vigorous dissent, the panel's majority expressly chose to avoid the issue of whether it would have reached the same result if the defendant had not agreed to pay for his sexual misconduct.[14] In another, it elected to construe the legislation narrowly and thereby avoided the necessity of ruling on the scope of Congress's power under the clause.[15] In a third, the court held that Congress's authority to regulate foreign commerce extended to the regulation of the channels of U.S. foreign commerce; it left for another day the questions of whether the domestic "affect on commerce" prerogative has a foreign commerce counterpart or whether foreign commerce issues should be judged by standards of their own.[16]

Congress has resorted on countless occasions to its authority to enact extraterritorial legislation not only in reliance on its own enumerated powers but also, reliance on the powers vested in one of the other branches or on powers it shares with one of the other branches – through the necessary and proper clause.[17] It has, for instance, regularly called upon the authority deposited with the President and the Congress in the fields of foreign affairs and military activities,[18] powers which the courts have described in particularly sweeping terms.[19]

Constitutional Limitations

Nevertheless, the powers granted by the Constitution are not without limit.[20] The clauses enumerating Congress's powers carry specific and implicit limits which govern the extent to which the power may be exercised overseas.[21] Other limitations appear elsewhere in the Constitution, most notably in the due process clauses of the Fifth Amendment.[22] Some limitations are a product of the need to harmonize potentially conflicting grants of authority. For example, although the Constitution reserves to the states the residue of governmental powers which it does not vest elsewhere, the primacy it affords the federal government in the area of foreign affairs limits the authority of the states in the field principally to those areas where they are acting with federal authority or acquiescence.[23]

In the area of extraterritorial jurisdiction, the most often cited limitation resides in the due process clause of the Fifth Amendment. While the enumerated powers may carry specific limits which govern the extent to which the power may be exercised overseas, the general restrictions of the Fifth Amendment due process clause have traditionally been mentioned as the most likely to define the outer reaches of the power to enact and enforce legislation with extraterritorial application.[24]

Unfortunately, many of the cases do little more than note that due process restrictions mark the frontier of the authority to enact and enforce American law abroad.[25] Even the value of this scant illumination is dimmed by the realization that the circumstances most likely to warrant such due process analysis are the very ones for which the least process is due. Although American courts that try aliens for overseas violations of American law must operate within the confines of due process,[26] the Supreme Court has observed that the Constitution's due process commands do not protect aliens who lack any "significant voluntary connection[s] with the United States."[27] Moreover, the Court's more recent decisions often begin with the assumption that the issues of extraterritorial jurisdiction come without constitutional implications.[28]

A handful, but growing number, of lower courts have considered due process issues. Some describe a due process requirement that demands some nexus between the United States and the circumstances of the offense.[29] In some instances, they look to international law principles to provide a useful measure to determine whether the nexus requirement has been met;[30] in others they consider the principles at work in the minimum contacts test for personal jurisdiction.[31] At the heart of these cases is the notion that due process expects that a defendant's conduct must have some past, present, or anticipated locus or impact within the United States before he can fairly be held criminal liable for it in an American court. The commentators have greeted this analysis with some hesitancy,[32] and some courts have simply rejected it.[33]

A related due process challenge is based on notice. It is akin to the concerns over secret laws and vague statutes, the exception to the maxim that ignorance of the law is no defense.[34] Here, indicia of knowledge, of reason to know, of an obligation to know, or of reasonable ignorance of the law's requirements – some of which are reflected in international standards – seem to be the most relevant factors. Citizens, for instance, might be expected to know the laws of their own nation; seafarers to know the law of the sea and consequently the laws of the nation under which they sail; everyone should be aware of the laws of the land in which they find themselves and of the wrongs condemned by the laws of all nations.[35] On the other hand, the application of American criminal statute to an alien in a foreign country under whose laws the conduct is lawful would seem to evidence a lack of notice sufficient to raise due process concerns.[36]

Conceding this outer boundary, however, the courts fairly uniformly have held that questions of extraterritoriality are almost exclusively within the discretion of Congress; a determination to grant a statutory provision extraterritorial application – regardless of its policy consequences – is not by itself constitutionally suspect.

Statutory Construction

For this reason, the question of the extent to which a particular statute applies outside the United States has generally been considered a matter of statutory, rather than constitutional, construction.[37] General rules of statutory construction have emerged which can explain, if not presage, the result in a given case. The first of these holds that a statute that is silent on the question of overseas application will be construed to have only territorial application unless there is a clear indication of some broader intent.[38]

A second rule of construction states that the nature and purpose of a statute may provide an indication of whether Congress intended a statute to apply beyond the confines of the United States. Although hints of it can be found earlier,[39] the rule was first clearly announced in *United States v. Bowman.*[40]

Does the Supreme Court's emphatic endorsement of the domestic presumption in a civil context in *Morrison v. National Australia Bank Ltd.*[41] cast doubt on Bowman's continued vitality? Early indications are that the courts and commentators are unwilling to go that far.[42]

The final rule declares that unless a contrary intent is clear, Congress is assumed to have acted so as not to invite action inconsistent with international law.[43] At one time, the cases seemed to imply the existence of another rule, that is, unless Congress declared that it intended a statute to apply overseas to both aliens and American nationals, it would be presumed to apply only to Americans.[44] In the eyes of the community of nations, a jurisdictional claim over misconduct based solely on the nationality of the victim continues to be among the more tenuous. Yet as discussed below, the challenge seems less compelling in light of the generous reading of the internationally recognized grounds upon which to stake a claim.[45]

International Law

International law supports rather than dictates decisions in the area of the overseas application of American law. Neither Congress nor the courts are bound to the dictates of international law when enacting or interpreting statutes with extraterritorial application.[46]

Yet Congress looks to international law when it evaluates the policy considerations associated with legislation that may have international consequences. For this reason, the courts interpret legislation with the presumption that Congress or the state legislature intends its laws to be applied within the bounds of international law, unless it indicates otherwise.

To what extent does international law permit a nation to exercise extraterritorial criminal jurisdiction? The question is essentially one of national interests. What national interest is served by extraterritorial application and what interests of other nations suffer by an extraterritorial application?

The most common classification of these interests dates to a 1935 Harvard Law School study which divided them into five categories or principles corresponding to the circumstances under which the nations of the world had declared their criminal laws applicable: (1) the territorial principle which involves crimes occurring or having an impact within the territory of a country; (2) the nationality principle which involves crimes committed by its nationals; (3) the passive personality principle which involves crimes committed against its nationals; (4) the protection principle which involves the crimes which have an impact on its interests as a nation; and (5) the universal principle which involves crimes which are universally condemned.[47]

The American Law Institute's Third Restatement of the Foreign Relations Law of the United States contains perhaps the most comprehensive, contemporary statement of international law in the area. It indicates that reasonableness defines the latitude that international law affords a country to enact, try, and punish violations of its law extraterritorially; its assessment of reasonableness mirrors a balancing of the interests represented in the Harvard study principles.[48]

While the Restatement's views carry considerable weight with both Congress and the courts,[49] the courts have traditionally ascertained the extent to which international law would recognize extraterritorial application of a particular law by citing the Harvard study principles, read expansively.[50]

The territorial principle of the Harvard study principles applies more widely than its title might suggest. It covers conduct within a nation's geographical borders. Yet, it also encompasses laws governing conduct on its territorial waters, conduct on its vessels on the high seas, conduct committed only in part within its geographical boundaries, and conduct elsewhere that has an impact within its territory.[51] Congress often indicates within the text of a statute when it intends a provision to apply within its territorial waters and upon its vessels.[52] Although rarely mentioned in the body of a statute, the courts have long and regularly acknowledged the "impact" basis for a claim of extraterritorial application.[53] This is particularly so, when the facts in a case suggest other principles of international law in addition to the territorial principle.[54]

If the territorial principle is more expansive than its caption might imply, the protective principle is less so. It is confined to crimes committed outside a nation's territory against its "security, territorial integrity or political independence."[55] As construed by the courts, however, it is understood to permit the application abroad of statutes which protect the federal government and its functions.[56] And so, it covers the overseas murder or attempted murder of federal officers or those thought to be federal officers;[57] acts of terrorism calculated to influence American foreign policy;[58] conduct which Congress has characterized as a threat to U.S. national security;[59] false statements or forgery designed to frustrate the administration of U.S. immigration law;[60] entering the United States as a stowaway;[61] or overseas bribery in connection with the award of federal government contracts.[62]

The nationality principle rests the exercise of extraterritorial criminal jurisdiction on the citizenship of accused.[63] It is the principle mirrored in the Supreme Court's statements in *Blackmer*, following the contempt conviction of an American living in Paris who ignored a federal court subpoena.[64] As in the case of *Blackmer*, which evidenced both the nationality and the protective principles, cases involving the nationality principle often involve other principles as well.[65]

The passive personality principle recognizes extraterritorial criminal jurisdiction based on the nationality of the victim of the offense.[66] It, too, has been asserted most often in the presence of facts suggesting other principles.[67]

The universal principle is based on the premise that offenses against all nations may be punished by any nation where the offender is found.[68] At a minimum, it applies to piracy and offenses committed on the high seas on "stateless" vessels.[69]

Current Extent of American Extraterritorial Criminal Jurisdiction

Federal Law

Express

Congress's declaration that a particular statute is to apply outside of the United States is the most obvious evidence of an intent to create extraterritorial jurisdiction.[70] Congress has expressly provided for the extraterritorial application of federal criminal law most often by outlawing various forms of misconduct when they occur "within the special maritime and territorial jurisdiction of the United States."[71] The concept of special maritime and territorial jurisdiction, if not the phrase, dates from the First Congress,[72] and encompasses navigable waters and federal enclaves within the United States as well as areas beyond the territorial confines of the United States. Although the concept of the special maritime and territorial jurisdiction of the United States once embraced little more than places over which the United States enjoyed state-like legislative jurisdiction, U.S. navigable territorial waters, and vessels of the United States, its application has been statutorily expanded. It now supplies an explicit basis for the extraterritorial application of various federal criminal laws relating to:

- air travel (special aircraft jurisdiction of the United States);[73]
- customs matters (customs waters of the U.S.);[74]
- U.S. spacecraft in flight;[75]
- evasive, stateless submersible vessels on the high seas;[76]
- overseas federal facilities and overseas residences of federal employees;[77]
- members of U.S. armed forces overseas and those accompanying them;[78]
- overseas human trafficking and sex offenses by federal employees, U.S. military personnel, or those accompanying them.[79]

The obligations and principles of various international treaties, conventions, or agreements to which the United States is a party supply the theme for a second category of federal criminal statutes with explicit extraterritorial application.[80] The range of these treaty-based federal crimes differs. Some have extraterritorial application only when the offender is an American.[81] Some address misconduct so universally condemned that they fall within federal jurisdiction regardless of any other jurisdictional considerations as long as the offender flees to the United States, is brought here for prosecution, or is otherwise "found in the United States" after the commission of the offense.[82] Some enjoy extraterritorial application under any of a number of these and other explicit jurisdictional circumstances.[83]

Members of another category of explicit extraterritorial federal criminal statutes either cryptically declare that their provisions are to apply overseas[84] or describe a series of jurisdictional circumstances under which their provisions have extraterritorial application, not infrequently involving the foreign commerce of the United States in conjunction with other factors.[85]

Maritime Drug Law Enforcement Act

The Maritime Drug Law Enforcement Act (MDLEA) is somewhat unusual in that it expressly authorizes extraterritorial coverage of federal criminal law predicated on nothing more than the consent of the nation with primary criminal jurisdiction.[86] MDLEA outlaws the manufacture, distribution, or possession with intent to manufacture or distribute controlled substances aboard vessels within the jurisdiction of the United States.[87] It defines vessels within the jurisdiction of the United States not only in terms of ordinary U.S. maritime jurisdiction, but envelops the maritime jurisdiction of other countries as long as they have consented to the application of the U.S. law aboard the vessel.[88] The definition also encompasses "vessels without nationality" sometimes referred to as "stateless" vessels, that is, vessels for which no national registry is effectively claimed.[89]

MDLEA provides the basis for Coast Guard drug interdiction efforts in the Caribbean and in the eastern Pacific off the coast of Central and South America.[90] The courts have concluded that MDLEA constitutes a valid exercise of Congress's constitutional authority to define and punish offenses against the law of nations, U.S. Const. Art. I, §8, cl.10.[91] They are divided over whether the prosecution must show some nexus between the United States and the offense[92] and over the application of the subsection of the act that assigns jurisdictional determinations to the court rather than to the jury, 46 U.S.C. 70504(a).[93]

Implied

The natural implications of *Bowman* [94] and Ford [95] are that a substantial number of other federal crimes operate overseas by virtue of the implicit intent of Congress. In fact, the lower federal courts have read *Bowman and Ford* to suggest that American extraterritorial criminal jurisdiction includes a wide range of statutes designed to protect federal officers, employees and property, to prevent smuggling and to deter the obstruction or corruption of the overseas activities of federal departments and agencies.[96] They have held, for instance, that the statute outlawing the assassination of Members of Congress may be applied against an American for a murder committed in a foreign country,[97] and that statutes prohibiting the murder or kidnaping of federal law enforcement officials apply in other countries even if the offenders are not Americans,[98] and even if the offenders incorrectly believed the victims were federal law enforcement officers.[99] They have also considered extraterritorial jurisdiction appropriate to (1) cases where aliens have attempted to defraud the United States in order to gain admission into the United States;[100] (2) false statements made by Americans overseas;[101] (3) the theft of federal property abroad;[102] (4) counterfeiting, forging or otherwise misusing federal documents or checks overseas by either Americans or aliens;[103] and (5) murder of a foreign national in another nation designed to facilitate the operation of a criminal enterprise in the United States.[104]

A logical extension would be to conclude that statutes enacted to prevent and punish the theft of federal property apply world-wide. And there seems to be no obvious reason why statutes protecting the United States from intentional deprivation of its property by destruction should be treated differently than those where the loss is attributable to theft.[105]

Finally, there are the "piggyback statutes" whose provisions are necessarily related to some other crime. An individual may be guilty of conspiracy to violate a federal law within the United States notwithstanding the fact he never enters the United States; it is sufficient that he is a member of a conspiracy to violate the American law.[106] The rationale should apply with equal force to the case of any accessory to the violation of any federal crime.[107] Nevertheless, a few recent statutes make the coverage of piggyback offenses explicit.[108]

A number of statutes condemn both a substantive offense and the piggy-back crimes (conspiracy or attempt) associated with the substantive offense. A statute which applies overseas carries with it the application of provisions which prohibit attempts or conspiracies to violate the underlying statute.[109]

State Law

State criminal laws are less likely to apply overseas than federal laws.[110] State law produces fewer instances where a statute was clearly enacted with an eye to its application overseas and fewer examples where frustration of legislative purpose is the logical consequence of purely territorial application. The Constitution seems to have preordained this result when it vested responsibility for protecting American interests and fulfilling American responsibilities overseas in the federal government.[111]

The primacy of the federal government in foreign affairs might suggest that the Constitution precludes the application of state law in other countries, but the courts and commentators have recognized a limited power of the states to enact law governing conduct outside the United States.[112] Obviously, Congress may, by preemptive action, extinguish the legislative authority of a state in any area over which Congress has plenary powers. And the Supremacy Clause also renders treaties to which the United States is a party binding upon the states and therefore beyond their legislative reach.[113] The constitutional limitations aside and in the absence of federal legislative action, however, "the question ... is one of whether the state actually intended to legislate extraterritorially, not whether it has the power to do so."[114]

The states have chosen to make their laws applicable beyond their boundaries in only a limited set of circumstances and ordinarily only in cases where there is some clear nexus to the state.[115] Perhaps the most common state statutory provision claiming state extraterritorial criminal jurisdiction is one which asserts jurisdiction in cases where some of the elements of the offense are committed within the state or others are committed outside it.[116] Another common claim is where an individual outside the state attempts or conspires to commit a crime within the state;[117] or one within the state attempts or conspires to commit a crime beyond its boundaries.[118] Still others define the state's extraterritorial jurisdiction to include instances where the victim of homicide, fatally wounded outside of the state, dies within it;[119] where property stolen elsewhere is brought into the state;[120] or where conduct outside the state constitutes the failure to comply with a legal duty imposed by state law.[121]

Investigation and Prosecution

Although a substantial number of federal criminal statutes have undisputed extraterritorial scope and a great many more have apparent extraterritorial range, prosecutions are few. Investigators and prosecutors face legal, practical, and often diplomatic obstacles that can be daunting. Some of these are depicted in the description that follows of some of procedural aspects of the American investigation and prosecution of a crime committed abroad.

With respect to diplomatic concerns, the Restatement observes:

> It is universally recognized, as a corollary of state sovereignty, that officials of one state may not exercise their functions in the territory of another state without the latter's consent. Thus, while a state may take certain measures of nonjudicial enforcement against a person in another state, ... its law enforcement officers cannot arrest him in another state, and can engage in criminal investigation in that state only with that state's consent. RESTATEMENT (THIRD) OF FOREIGN RELATIONS LAW §432 cmt. b (1986).

Failure to comply can result in strong diplomatic protests, liability for reparations, and other remedial repercussions, to say nothing of the possible criminal prosecution of offending foreign investigators.[122] Consequently, investigations within another country of extraterritorial federal crimes without the consent or at least acquiescence of the host country are extremely rare.

Mutual Legal Assistance Treaties and Agreements

Congress has endorsed diplomatic efforts to increase multinational cooperative law enforcement activities. The United States has over 60 mutual legal assistance treaties in force.[123] Their benefits are typically available to state and federal law enforcement investigators though the Department of Justice's Office of International Affairs.[124] Initially negotiated to overcome impediments posed by foreign bank secrecy laws,[125] the treaties generally offer more than the collection and delivery of documents. They ordinarily provide similar clauses, with some variations, for locating and identifying persons and items;[126] service of process;[127] executing search warrants;[128] taking witness depositions;[129] persuading foreign nationals to come to the United States voluntarily to present evidence here;[130] and forfeiture-related seizures.[131]

Letters Rogatory

Witness depositions may be taken in a foreign country using letters rogatory. Letters rogatory involve the formal request from the courts of one country to those of another asking that a witness' statement be taken. The procedure is governed by statute and rule.[132] It is often a resource of last resort. The process, through diplomatic channels, is time consuming, cumbersome, and lies within the discretion of the foreign court to which it is addressed.[133]

Cooperative Efforts

American law enforcement officials have historically used other, often less formal, cooperative methods overseas to investigate and prosecute extraterritorial offenses.[134] Over the last few decades the United States has taken steps to facilitate cooperative efforts. In addition to the more traditional presence of members of the Armed Forces and the State Department personnel and contractors, federal civilian law enforcement agencies have assigned an increasing number of personnel overseas. For example, the Justice Department's Criminal Division has resident legal advisors in 37 countries abroad;[135] and the Federal Bureau of Investigation now operates legal attache offices in 75 foreign cities;[136] the Drug Enforcement Administration has offices in 85 cities overseas;[137] the U.S. Immigration and Customs Enforcement agency operates out of 70 locations;[138] the Secret Service has 20 such offices.[139]

A few regulatory agencies with law enforcement responsibilities have working arrangements with their foreign counterparts. The Securities and

Exchange Commission, for instance, has bilateral enforcement memoranda of understanding with 20 foreign securities commissions and, with 62 others, is a signatory of the International Organization of Securities Commissions' multilateral memorandum of understanding (IOSCO MMOU).[140]

Congress has enacted several measures to assign foreign law enforcement efforts in this country in anticipation of reciprocal treatment. For instance, the Foreign Evidence Request Efficiency Act of 2009 authorizes Justice Department attorneys to petition federal judges for any of a series of orders to facilitate investigations in this country by foreign law enforcement authorities.[141] The authorization extends to the issuance of:

- search warrants;
- court orders for access to stored electronic communications and to communications records;
- pen register or trap and trace orders; and
- subpoena authority, both testimonial and for the production of documents and other material.[142]

Search and Seizure Abroad

Overseas cooperative law enforcement assistance occasionally has either Fourth or Fifth Amendment implications. In the case of the Fourth Amendment, the relatively limited lower federal court case law has remained fairly uniform, although the diversity of views reflected in the Supreme Court's *Verdugo-Urquidez* decision in 1990[143] lends an air of uncertainty to the matter. Prior to *Verdugo-Urquidez*, it seems to have been generally agreed that the Fourth Amendment governed the overseas search and seizure of the person or property of Americans by American law enforcement officials.[144] On the other hand, neither the Fourth Amendment[145] nor its exclusionary rule[146] were considered applicable to overseas searches and seizures conducted by foreign law enforcement officials,[147] except under two circumstances. The first exception covered foreign conduct which "shocked the conscience of the court."[148] The second reached foreign searches or seizures in which American law enforcement officials were so deeply involved as to constitute "joint ventures" or some equivalent level of participation.[149] The cases seldom explained whether these exceptions operated under all circumstances or only when searches or seizures involved the person or property of Americans. In the days when MLATs were scarce, however, the courts rarely, if ever, encountered circumstances sufficient to activate either exception.

Verdugo-Urquidez may suggest a more narrow application of the Fourth Amendment than was previously contemplated. It holds that "the Fourth Amendment [does not] appl[y] to the search and seizure by United States agents of property that is owned by a nonresident alien and located in a foreign country," 494 U.S. at 261. The majority opinion is grounded not in the principles previously announced by the lower courts but in its reading of the history of the Amendment and of the Court's earlier treatment of the Constitution's application overseas and to aliens.[150] Earlier lower court jurisprudence is neither mentioned nor cited. Moreover, one of the Justices in the five member majority and a sixth Justice authored concurrences in which they indicated that Fourth Amendment reasonableness abroad may be very different from the Amendment's demands domestically.[151]

One commentator argues that the concurrences should be read as confining rather than expanding the impact of the majority decision:

> Given *Verdugo-Urquidez*, it might understandably be thought that the issue discussed herein – when, if ever, a United States connection with a search in a foreign country is substantial enough to make the Fourth Amendment and its exclusionary rule applicable – is of no relevance whenever that search is directed at an alien not then in the United States. But, an examination of the positions of the two concurring and three dissenting Justices suggests otherwise. The dissenters ... are of the view that if the foreign search is properly characterized as United States activity ... then the Fourth Amendment applies if the defendant is being subjected to a U.S. criminal prosecution.... Thus, the *most* that can be definitely concluded from *Verdugo-Urquidez* is that the Fourth Amendment's warrant clause is inapplicable to a search conducted under the circumstances present in that case. Beyond that, much depends upon the exact positions of the two [cryptic] concurring Justices. 1 LaFave, SEARCH AND SEIZURE: A TREATISE ON THE FOURTH AMENDMENT 325-26 (4th ed. 2004)(emphasis in the original).

Subsequent case law in the lower federal courts acknowledges *Verdugo-Urquidez* and molds the principles of the opinion for the Court into the body of pre-existing law. Although limited, it indicates that the Fourth Amendment does not apply to a search conducted overseas of the property of a foreign national with no voluntary connection to the United States.[152] As for overseas searches of the property of Americans or aliens permanently resident in the United States, the Fourth Amendment is said not to apply to a search by foreign officials unless conducted as a "joint venture" with American authorities or unless the conduct of the foreign officials "shocks the conscience of the court."[153] Nevertheless, "the Fourth Amendment's reasonableness standard applies to United States officials conducting a search affecting a United States citizen in a foreign country."[154] On the other hand, even under such circumstances, "a foreign search is reasonable if it conforms to the requirements of foreign law," and "such a search will be upheld under the good faith exception to the exclusionary rule when United States officials reasonably rely on foreign officials' representations of foreign law."[155]

Self-Incrimination Overseas

Like the Fourth Amendment protection against unreasonable searches and seizures, the Fifth Amendment self-incrimination clause and its attendant *Miranda* warning requirements do not apply to statements made overseas to foreign officials[156] subject to the same "joint venture"[157] and "shocked conscience" exceptions.[158] The Fifth Amendment and *Miranda* requirements do apply to custodial interrogations conducted overseas by American officials regardless of the nationality of the defendant.[159] Of course as a general rule to be admissible at trial in this country, any confession must have been freely made.[160]

Statute of Limitations: 18 U.S.C. 3292 and Related Matters

As a general rule, prosecution of federal crimes must begin within five years.[161] Federal capital offenses, certain federal sex offenses, and certain violent federal terrorist offenses, however, may be prosecuted at any time.[162] Prosecution of nonviolent federal terrorism offenses must begin within eight years.[163] Moreover, the statute of limitations is suspended or tolled during any period in which the accused is a fugitive.[164]

Whatever the applicable statute of limitations, section 3292 authorizes the federal courts to suspend it in order to await the arrival of evidence requested of a foreign government:

> Upon application of the United States, filed before return of an indictment, indicating that evidence of an offense is in a foreign country, the district court before which a grand jury is impaneled to investigate the offense shall suspend the running of the statute of limitations for the offense if the court finds by a preponderance of the evidence that an official request has been made for such evidence and that it reasonably appears, or reasonably appeared at the time the

request was made, that such evidence is, or was, in such foreign country. 18 U.S.C. 3292(a)(1).

Section 3292 suspensions may run for no more than six months if the requested foreign assistance is provided before the time the statute of limitations would otherwise have expired and for no more than three years in other instances.[165] The suspension period begins with the filing of the request for foreign assistance and ends with final action by the foreign government upon the request.[166] The government must show by a preponderance of the evidence that the purpose of the request is to obtain evidence located overseas.[167] Because of the built-in time limits, however, the government need not show that it acted diligently in its attempts to gather overseas evidence.[168] The circuits are divided over whether the section may be used to revive a statute of limitations by filing a request after the statute has run,[169] and over whether the section can be used to extend the statute of limitations with respect to evidence that the government has already received at the time it filed the request.[170] At least one circuit has held that the statutory reference to "the district court before which a grand jury is impaneled to investigate the offense" is intended to identify the court that may issue the suspension order and does not limit the statute to requests filed in aid of a pending grand jury investigation.[171]

Extradition

Extradition is perhaps the oldest form of international law enforcement assistance. It is a creature of treaty by which one country surrenders a fugitive to another for prosecution or service of sentence.[172] The United States has bilateral extradition treaties with roughly two-thirds of the nations of the world.[173] Treaties negotiated before 1960 and still in effect reflect the view then held by the United States and other common law countries that criminal jurisdiction was territorial and consequently extradition could not be had for extraterritorial crimes.[174] Subsequently negotiated agreements either require extradition regardless of where the offense occurs,[175] permit extradition regardless of where the offense occurs,[176] or require extradition where the extraterritorial laws of the two nations are compatible.[177]

More recent extradition treaties address other traditional features of the nation's earlier agreements that complicate extradition, most notably the nationality exception, the political offense exception, and the practice of limiting extradition to a list of specifically designated offenses.

Federal crimes committed within other countries are more likely to be the work of foreign nationals than is otherwise the case. Yet, the "most common type of treaty provision provides that neither of the contracting parties shall be bound to deliver up its own citizens or subjects."[178] Most treaties negotiated of late, however, contain either an article declaring that extradition may not be denied on the basis of nationality[179] or one declaring that if extradition is denied on the basis of nationality the case must be referred to local authorities for prosecution.[180]

"The political offense exception is now a standard clause in almost all extradition treaties of the world."[181] Originally designed to protect unsuccessful insurgents in flight,[182] it is often construed to include both the purely political offense such as treason and sedition and related political offenses such as an act of violence committed during the course of, and in furtherance of, a political upheaval.[183] The exception is somewhat at odds with contemporary desires to prevent, prosecute, and punish acts of terrorism. Consequently, treaties forged over the last several years frequently include some form of limitation on the exception, often accompanied by a discretionary right to refuse politically or otherwise discriminatorily motivated extradition requests.[184]

Current U.S. extradition treaties signed prior to the 1980's list specific crimes to which the treaty is limited.[185] In the nation's first extradition treaty the list was limited to murder and forgery;[186] towards the end of the twentieth century the standard lists had grown to close to or more than thirty crimes.[187] Treaties agreed to more recently opt for a generic description.[188]

As an alternative to extradition, particularly if the suspect is not a citizen of the country of refuge, foreign authorities may be willing to expel or deport him under circumstances that allow the United States to take him into custody.[189] In the absence of a specific treaty provision, the fact that the defendant was abducted overseas and brought to the United States for trial rather than pursuant to a request under the applicable extradition treaty does not deprive the federal court of jurisdiction to try him.[190]

Venue

Federal crimes committed within the United States must be tried where they occur.[191] Venue over extraterritorial crimes is a matter of statute, 18 U.S.C. 3238. Section 3238 permits the trial of extraterritorial crimes either (1) in the district into which the offender is "first brought" or in which he is arrested for the offense; or (2) prior to that time, by indictment or information in the district of the offender's last known residence, or if none is known, in the District of Columbia.[192] The phrase "first brought" as used in section 3238 means "first brought while in custody."[193] As the language of the section suggests, venue for all joint offenders is proper wherever venue for one of their number is proper.[194] Courts are divided over whether section 3238 may be applied even though venue may have been proper without recourse to its provisions.[195]

Testimony of Overseas Witnesses

A federal court may subpoena a United States resident or national found abroad to appear before it or the grand jury.[196] Federal courts ordinarily have no authority to subpoena foreign nationals located in a foreign country.[197] Mutual legal assistance treaties and similar agreements generally contain provisions to facilitate a transfer of custody of foreign witnesses who are imprisoned overseas[198] and in other instances to elicit assistance to encourage foreign nationals to come to this country and testify voluntarily.[199]

Unable to secure the presence of overseas witnesses, federal courts may authorize depositions to be taken abroad, under "exceptional circumstances and in the interests of justice"[200] under even more limited circumstances, they may admit such depositions into evidence in a criminal trial.

Originally, only a defendant might request that depositions be taken under Rule 15 of the Federal Rules of Criminal Procedure,[201] but they have been available to prosecutors since the 1970s.[202] The Rule offers depositions as an alternative to long term incarceration of material witnesses.[203] Otherwise, depositions may be ordered only under exceptional circumstances. Some courts have said that to "establish exceptional circumstances the moving party must show the witness's unavailability and the materiality of the witness's testimony."[204] Others would add to these that "the testimony is necessary to prevent a failure of justice" or additional considerations.[205] In any event, once a deposition has been taken the impediments to its use at trial, especially by the prosecution, are much more formidable.

"Compliance with Rule 15 is a necessary but not sufficient condition for use of a deposition at trial."[206] Admissibility at trial requires compliance with Rule 15, the Federal Rules of Evidence, and the Constitution's confrontation clause. As general matter, depositions are to be taken in the same manner as depositions in civil cases.[207] Moreover, the Rule requires that the defendant be afforded an opportunity to attend depositions taken at the government's request.[208] The requirement reflects the demands of the Constitution's confrontation clause: "In all criminal prosecutions, the accused shall enjoy the right ... to be confronted with the witnesses against him," U.S. Const. Amend.

VI. The right embodies not only the prerogative of a literal face to face confrontation, but also the right to cross examine and to have the witness's testimonial demeanor exposed to the jury.[209]

In the case of depositions taken overseas, the courts have observed that the right to confrontation is not absolute.[210] When a deposition is taken abroad, the courts prefer that the defendant be present,[211] that his counsel be allowed to cross-examine the witness,[212] that the deposition be taken under oath,[213] that a verbatim transcript be taken, and that the deposition be captured on videotape;[214] but they have permitted depositions to be admitted into evidence at subsequent criminal trials in this country, notwithstanding the fact that one or more of these optimal conditions are not present.[215] In some of those nations whose laws might not otherwise require or even permit depositions under conditions considered preferable under U.S. law, a treaty provision addresses the issue.[216]

The Federal Rules of Evidence govern the admissibility of evidence in federal criminal trials. A deposition taken overseas that has survived Rule 15 and confrontation clause scrutiny is likely to be found admissible. The hearsay rule, Rule 802 which reflects the law's preference for evidence that is exposed to the adversarial process, poses the most obvious obstacle.[217] The Rules, however, provide an explicit exception for depositions,[218] one that has been applied to depositions taken overseas under the authority of Rule 15.[219]

Yet the question of admissibility of overseas depositions rests ultimately upon whether the confrontation clause demands can be satisfied. The cases thus far have relied upon the Supreme Court's decisions either in *Ohio v. Roberts*[220] or in *Maryland v. Craig*.[221] Faced with the question of whether trial witnesses might testify remotely via a two-way video conference, *Craig* held that the confrontation clause's requirement of physical face-to-face confrontation between witness and defendant at trial can be excused under limited circumstances in light of "considerations of public policy and necessities of the case."[222] *Roberts* dealt with the question of whether the admission of hearsay evidence violated the confrontation clause, and declared that as long as the hearsay evidence came within a "firmly rooted hearsay exception" its admission into evidence in a criminal trial constituted no breach of the clause.[223]

More recent decisions might be thought to call into question any continued reliance on *Roberts* and *Craig*. At a minimum, the Supreme Court's *Crawford v. Washington* opinion repudiates the suggestion that *Roberts* permits anything less than actual confrontation in the case of "testimonial" hearsay, for example, a formal statement to a government official, such as an affidavit or other pretrial statement.[224] At least one appellate panel has concluded that the prosecution's need for critical evidence does not alone supply the kind of public policy considerations necessary to qualify for a *Craig* exception;[225] but another has held that national security interests may suffice.[226]

Since the pre-*Crawford* cases required a good faith effort to assure the defendant's attendance at overseas depositions, it might be argued that *Crawford* requires no adjustment in the area's jurisprudence. Moreover, the Eleventh Circuit en banc *Craig* analysis implied that it thought the use of overseas depositions at trial more compatible with the confrontation clause than the use of video trial testimony.[227] In addition, the Fourth Circuit rejected a confrontation clause challenge where the circumstances satisfied the dual demands for a *Craig* exception: (1) denial of a face to face confrontation made necessary by important policy considerations, and (2) assurance of reliability in the form of an "oath, cross-examination, and observation of the witness' demeanor."[228]

National Security Concerns

When witnesses and other evidence are located abroad, a defendant's statutory and constitutional rights may conflict with the government's need for secrecy for diplomatic and national security reasons. Rule 16 of the Federal Rules of Criminal Procedure entitles a defendant to disclosure of any of his statements in the government's possession, but the prosecution's case may have evolved from foreign intelligence gathering.[229] The Sixth Amendment assures a criminal defendant of "compulsory process for obtaining witnesses in his favor," but providing a witness who is also a terrorist suspect and in federal custody may have an adverse impact on the witness's value as an intelligence source.[230] The Sixth Amendment promises a criminal defendant the right to confront the witnesses against him, even a witness who presents classified information to the jury.[231]

Congress has provided the Classified Information Procedures Act as a means of accommodating the conflict of interests.[232] The act permits the court to approve prosecution prepared summaries of classified information to be disclosed to the defendant and introduced in evidence, as a substitute for the classified information.[233] The summaries, however, must be an adequate replacement for the classified information, because ultimately the government's national security interests "cannot override the defendant's right to a fair trial."[234]

Admissibility of Foreign Documents

There is a statutory procedure designed to ease the evidentiary admission of foreign business records in federal courts, 18 U.S.C. 3505.[235] The section covers "foreign record[s] of regularly conducted activity" in virtually any form, i.e., any "memorandum, report, record, or data compilation, in any form, of acts, events, conditions, opinions, or diagnoses, maintained in a foreign country," 18 U.S.C. 3505(c)(1). It exempts qualified business records from the operation of the hearsay rule in federal criminal proceedings[236] and permits their authentication upon foreign certification.[237] Finally, it establishes a procedure under which the reliability of the documents can be challenged in conjunction with other pre-trial motions.[238] While the prosecution's failure to provide timely notice of its intent to rely upon section 3505 does not necessarily bar admission,[239] its failure to supply a foreign certification of authenticity precludes admission under the section.[240]

Early appellate decisions upheld section 3505 in the face of confrontation clause challenges, as in the case of depositions drawing support from *Ohio v. Roberts*.[241] As noted above, *Crawford* cast doubt upon the continued vitality of the *Roberts* rule (hearsay poses no confrontation problems as long as it falls within a "firmly rooted hearsay exception") when it held that only actual confrontation will suffice in the case of "testimonial" hearsay.[242] Although it left for another day a more complete definition of testimonial hearsay, *Crawford* did note in passing that "[m]ost of the hearsay exceptions covered statements that by their nature were not testimonial – for example business records."[243] More than one later court panel has rejected a confrontation clause challenge to section 3505 on the basis of this distinction.[244]

CONCLUSION

The Constitution grants Congress broad powers to enact laws of extraterritorial scope and imposes few limitations on the exercise of that power. The states enjoy only residual authority, but they too may and have enacted criminal laws which apply beyond the territorial confines of the United States. Prosecutions are relatively few, however, perhaps because of the practical, legal, and diplomatic obstacles that may attend such an endeavor.

ATTACHMENTS

Federal Criminal Laws Which Enjoy Express Extraterritorial Application

Special Maritime & Territorial Jurisdiction

8 U.S.C. 1375a(d)(3) (informed consent violations by international marriage brokers)

15 U.S.C. 1175 (manufacture or possession of gambling devices)

15 U.S.C. 1243 (manufacture or possession of switchblade knives)

15 U.S.C. 1245 (manufacture or possession of ballistic knives)

16 U.S.C. 3372(a)(3) (possession of illegally taken fish or wildlife)

18 U.S.C. 81 (arson)

18 U.S.C. 113 (assault)

18 U.S.C. 114 (maiming)

18 U.S.C. 115 (violence against federal officials, former officials and members of their families)

18 U.S.C. 117 (domestic assault by an habitual offender)

18 U.S.C. 118 (interference with certain protective functions [State Department & diplomatic security])

18 U.S.C. 249 (hate crimes)

18 U.S.C. 546 (smuggling goods into a foreign country from an American vessel)

18 U.S.C. 661 (theft)

18 U.S.C. 662 (receipt of stolen property)

18 U.S.C. 831 (threats, theft, or unlawful possession of nuclear material or attempting or conspiring to do so)

18 U.S.C. 1025 (false pretenses)

18 U.S.C. 1081 - 1083 (gambling ships)

18 U.S.C. 1111 (murder)

18 U.S.C. 1112 (manslaughter)

18 U.S.C. 1113 (attempted murder or manslaughter)

18 U.S.C. 1115 (misconduct or neglect by ship officers)

18 U.S.C. 1201 (kidnaping)

18 U.S.C. 1363 (malicious mischief)

18 U.S.C. 1460 (sale or possession with intent to sell obscene material)

18 U.S.C. 1466A (obscene visual representation of sexual abuse of children)

18 U.S.C. 1587 (captain of a slave vessel with slaves aboard)

18 U.S.C. 1591(sex trafficking of children)

18 U.S.C. 1656 (piratical conversion of vessel by captain, officer or crew member)

18 U.S.C. 1658 (plundering a ship in distress)

18 U.S.C. 1659 (attack upon a vessel with intent to plunder)

18 U.S.C. 1654 (Americans arming or serving on privateers outside the United States to be used against the United States or Americans)

18 U.S.C. 1801 (video voyeurism)

18 U.S.C. 1957 (prohibited monetary transactions)

18 U.S.C. 2111 (robbery)

18 U.S.C. 2191 (cruelty to seamen)

18 U.S.C. 2192 (incite to revolt or mutiny)

18 U.S.C. 2193 (revolt or mutiny by seamen)

18 U.S.C. 2194 (shanghaiing sailors)

18 U.S.C. 2195 (abandonment of sailors overseas)

18 U.S.C. 2196 (drunkenness of seamen)

18 U.S.C. 2197 (misuse of documents associated vessels)

18 U.S.C. 2198 (seduction of a female passenger)

18 U.S.C. 2199 (stowaways)

18 U.S.C. 2241 (aggravated sexual abuse)

18 U.S.C. 2242 (sexual abuse)

18 U.S.C. 2243 (sexual abuse of a minor or ward)

18 U.S.C. 2244 (abusive sexual contact)

18 U.S.C. 2252(a) (sale or possession of material involving sexual exploitation of children)

18 U.S.C. 2252A(a) (sale or possession of child pornography)

18 U.S.C. 2261 (interstate domestic violence)

18 U.S.C. 2261A (stalking)

18 U.S.C. 2262 (interstate violation of a protective order)

18 U.S.C. 2271-2279 (destruction of ships)

18 U.S.C. 2283 (transportation of explosives, biological, chemical, radioactive or nuclear materials for terrorist purposes on the high seas or aboard a U.S. vessel or in U.S. waters)

18 U.S.C. 2284 (transportation of a terrorist on the high seas or aboard a U.S. vessel or in U.S. waters)

18 U.S.C. 2318 (transporting counterfeit phonorecord labels, copies of computer programs or documentation, or copies of motion pictures or other audio visual works)

18 U.S.C. 2332b (acts of terrorism transcending national boundaries)

18 U.S.C. 2388 (war-time activities affecting armed forces)

18 U.S.C. 2422(b) (causing a minor to engage in prostitution or other sexual acts)

18 U.S.C. 2425 (transmission of information about a minor)

18 U.S.C. 3261(offenses committed by members of the United States armed forces or individuals accompanying or employed by the United States armed forces overseas)

46 U.S.C. 70503 (maritime drug law enforcement)

46 U.S.C. 70508 (operation of stateless submersible vessels)

48 U.S.C. 1912 (offenses committed on United States defense sites in the Marshall Islands or Federated States of Micronesia)

48 U.S.C.1934 (offenses committed on United States defense sites in Palau)

Special Aircraft Jurisdiction

18 U.S.C. 32 (destruction of aircraft)

18 U.S.C. 831 (threats, theft, or unlawful possession of nuclear material or attempting or conspiring to do so)

18 U.S.C. 1201 (kidnaping)

18 U.S.C. 2318 (transporting counterfeit phonorecord labels, copies of computer programs or documentation, or copies of motion pictures or other audio visual works)

49 U.S.C. 46502(a) (air piracy or attempted air piracy)

49 U.S.C. 46504 (interference with flight crew or attendants within the special aircraft jurisdiction of the United States)

49 U.S.C. 46506 (assaults, maiming, theft, receipt of stolen property, murder, manslaughter, attempted murder or manslaughter, robbery, or sexual abuse)

Treaty-Related

18 U.S.C. 32(b)

Offenses:

- violence aboard a foreign civil aircraft (likely to endanger the safety of the aircraft) while in flight;

- destruction of or incapacitating or endangering damage to foreign civil aircraft;
- placing a bomb aboard a foreign civil aircraft; or
- attempting or conspiring to do so

Jurisdictional factors:

- a United States national was on board;
- the offender was a United States national; or
- the offender is afterwards found in the United States

18 U.S.C. 37
Offenses:

- violence causing or likely to cause serious bodily injury or death at an international airport;
- destruction of or serious damage to aircraft or facilities at an international airport; or
- attempting or conspiring to do so

Jurisdictional factors:

- a victim was a United States national;
- the offender was a United States national; or
- the offender is afterwards found in the United States

18 U.S.C. 112
Offenses:

- assaulting an internationally protected person;
- threatening an internationally protected person; or
- attempting to threaten an internationally protected person

Jurisdictional factors:

- the victim was a United States national;
- the offender was a United States national; or
- the offender is afterwards found in the United States

18 U.S.C. 175
Offenses:

- develop, produce, stockpile, transfer, acquire, retain, or possess biological weapons or delivery systems, misuse of biological weapons;
- assisting a foreign power to do so; or
- attempting, threatening or conspiring to do so

Jurisdictional factor:

- "there is extraterritorial Federal jurisdiction over an offense under this section committed by or against a national of the United States," 18 U.S.C. 175(a)

18 U.S.C. 229
Offenses:

- using chemical weapons outside the United States; or
- attempting, or conspiring to do so

Jurisdictional factors:

- the victim or offender was a United States national; or
- the offense was committed against federal property

18 U.S.C. 831
Offenses:

- threats, theft, or unlawful possession of nuclear material; or
- attempting or conspiring to do so

Jurisdictional factors:

- a United States national or an American legal entity was the victim of the offense;
- the offender was a United States national or an American legal entity; or

- the offender is afterwards found in the United States;
- the offense involved a transfer to or from the United States; or
- the offense was a threat directed against the United States

18 U.S.C. 878
Offenses:

- threatening to assault, kill or kidnap an internationally protected person

Jurisdictional factors:

- the victim was a United States national;
- the offender was a United States national; or
- the offender is afterwards found in the United States

18 U.S.C. 1091
Offense: genocide

- killing members of a national, ethnic, racial or religious group
- assaulting members of a national, ethnic, racial or religious group
- imposing reproductive and other group destructive measures on a national, ethnic, racial or religious group
- forcibly transferring children of a national, ethnic, racial or religious group

Jurisdictional factors:

- the offender was a United States national
- the offender is a stateless person habitually residing in the United States
- the offender is present in the United States
- the offense occurred in part in the United States

18 U.S.C. 1116

- *Offense*: killing an internationally protected person

Jurisdictional factors:

- the victim was a United States national;
- the offender was a United States national; or
- the offender is afterwards found in the United States

18 U.S.C. 1117
Offense: conspiracy to kill an internationally protected person
Jurisdictional factors:

- the victim was a United States national;
- the offender was a United States national; or
- the offender is afterwards found in the United States

18 U.S.C. 1201
Offense:

- kidnaping an internationally protected person; or
- attempting or conspiring to do so

Jurisdictional factors:

- the victim was a United States national;
- the offender was a United States national; or
- the offender is afterwards found in the United States

18 U.S.C. 1203
Offense:

- hostage taking; or
- attempting or conspiring to do so

Jurisdictional factors:

- the victim was a United States national;
- the offender was a United States national; or
- the offender is afterwards found in the United States

18 U.S.C. 2280
Offenses:

- violence committed against maritime navigation; or
- attempting or conspiracy to commit violence against maritime navigation

Jurisdictional factors:

- the victim was a United States national;
- the offender was a United States national;
- the offender is afterwards found in the United States; or
- the offense was intended to compel action or abstention by the United States

18 U.S.C. 2281
Offenses:

- violence committed against a maritime platform; or
- attempting or conspiracy to commit violence against a maritime platform

Jurisdictional factors:

- the victim was a United States national;
- the offender was a United States national;
- the offender is afterwards found in the United States; or
- the offense was intended to compel action or abstention by the United States

18 U.S.C. 2332a
Offenses:

- using a weapon of mass destruction outside the United States; or
- threatening, attempting, or conspiring to do so

Jurisdictional factors:

- the victim was a United States national;
- the offender was a United States national; or
- the offense was committed against federal property

18 U.S.C. 2332f (effective upon the terrorist bombing convention entering into force for the U.S.)

Offenses:

- bombing public places, government facilities, or public utilities outside the United States; or
- threatening, attempting, or conspiring to do so

Jurisdictional factors:

- the victim was a United States national;
- the offender was a United States national;
- the offense was committed against federal property;
- the offender is present in the United States;
- the offense was committed on United States registered vessel or aircraft; or
- the offense was intended to compel action or abstention by the United States

18 U.S.C. 2339C

Offenses:

- financing terrorism outside the U.S.; or
- attempting or conspiring to do so

Jurisdictional factors:

- predicate act of terrorism was directed against
    - United States property,
    - United States nationals or their property, or

    - property of entities organized under United States law;
- offense was committed on United States registered vessel or aircraft operated by the United States.;
- the offense was intended to compel action or abstention by the United States;
- the offender was a United States national; or
- (effective upon the terrorism financing convention entering into force for the U.S.) the offender is present in the United States

18 U.S.C. 2340A
Offenses:

- torture under color of law outside the United States; or
- attempted torture

Jurisdictional factors:

- the offender was a United States national; or
- the offender is present in the United States

18 U.S.C. 2441
Offense:

- war crimes

Jurisdictional factors:

- an American or member of the American armed forces was the victim of the offense; or
- the offender was an American or member of the American armed forces

49 U.S.C. 46502(b)
Offenses:

- air piracy outside the special aircraft jurisdiction of the United States; or

- attempted air piracy outside the special aircraft jurisdiction of the United States

Jurisdictional factors:

- a United States national was aboard;
- the offender was a United States national; or
- the offender is afterwards found in the United States

Others

18 U.S.C. 175c (variola virus (small pox))
Jurisdictional factors:

- the offender or victim was a United States national;
- the offense occurred in or affected interstate or foreign commerce
- the offense was committed against U.S. property; or
- the offender aided or abetted the commission of an offense under the section for which there was extraterritorial jurisdiction

Attempt/conspiracy

- includes attempts and conspiracies

18 U.S.C. 351
Offenses:

- killing, kidnaping, attempting or conspiring to kill or kidnap, or assaulting a Member of Congress, a Supreme Court Justice, or senior executive branch official

Jurisdictional factors:

- "[t]here is extraterritorial jurisdiction over an offense prohibited by this section," 18 U.S.C. 351(i)

18 U.S.C. 877 (mailing threatening communications to the United States from foreign countries)

18 U.S.C. 956 (conspiracy and overt act within the United States to commit murder, kidnaping, maiming or the destruction of certain property overseas)

18 U.S.C. 1029

Offenses:

- fraud related to access devices; or
- attempting or conspiring to commit the offense

Jurisdictional factors:

- involves a device issued, managed or controlled by an entity within the jurisdiction of the United States and
- item used in the offense or proceeds are transported or transmitted to or through the United States or deposited here, 18 U.S.C. 1029(h)

18 U.S.C. 1119 (killing of American by an American in a foreign country)

18 U.S.C. 1204 (parental kidnaping by retaining a child outside the United States)

18 U.S.C. 1512

Offenses:

- tampering with a federal witness or informant; or
- attempting to tamper with a federal witness or informant

Jurisdictional factors:

- "[t]here is extraterritorial Federal jurisdiction over an offense under this section," 18 U.S.C. 1512(g)

18 U.S.C. 1513

Offenses:

- retaliating against a federal witness or informant; or
- attempting to retaliate against a federal witness or informant

Jurisdictional factors:

- "[t]here is extraterritorial Federal jurisdiction over an offense under this section," 18 U.S.C. 1513(d)

18 U.S.C. 1585 (service aboard a slave vessel by an American or American resident)

18 U.S.C. 1586 (service aboard a vessel transporting slaves from one foreign country to another by an American or American resident)

18 U.S.C. 1587 (captain of a slave vessel hovering off the coast of the United States)

18 U.S.C. 1596

Offenses:

- peonage (18 U.S.C. 1581)
- enticement into slavery (18 U.S.C. 1583)
- sale into involuntary servitude (18 U.S.C. 1584)
- forced labor (18 U.S.C. 1589)
- trafficking in re peonage, slavery, involuntary servitude, or forced labor (18 U.S.C. 1590)
- sex trafficking (18 U.S.C. 1591)

Jurisdictional factors:

- the offender is a United States national
- the offender is found in the United States

18 U.S.C. 1651 (piracy upon the high seas where the offender is afterwards brought into or found in the United States)

18 U.S.C. 1652 (Americans acting as privateers against the United States or Americans on the high seas)

18 U.S.C. 1653 (acts of piracy upon the high seas committed against the United States or Americans by aliens)

18 U.S.C. 1654 (Americans arming or serving on privateers outside the United States to be used against the United States or Americans)

18 U.S.C. 1751
Offenses:

- killing, kidnaping, attempting or conspiring to kill or kidnap, or assaulting the President, Vice President, or a senior White House official

Jurisdictional factors:

- "[t]here is extraterritorial jurisdiction over an offense prohibited by this section," 18 U.S.C. 1751(k)

18 U.S.C. 1831-1839
Offenses:

- economic espionage;
- theft of trade secrets

Jurisdictional factors:

- "[t]his chapter also applies to conduct occurring outside the United States if"
  (1) the offender was a United States national or entity organized under United States law; or
  (2) an act in furtherance was committed here, 18 U.S.C. 1837

18 U.S.C. 1956
Offense:

- money laundering

Jurisdictional factors: "[t]here is extraterritorial jurisdiction over the conduct prohibited by this section if

- the conduct is by a United States citizen or, in the case of a non-United States citizen, the conduct occurs in part in the United States; and
- the transaction or series of related transactions involves funds ... of a value exceeding $10,000," 18 U.S.C. 1956(f)

18 U.S.C. 1957
Offense:

- prohibited monetary transactions

Jurisdictional factors:

- the offense under this section takes place outside the United States, but the defendant is a United States person [other than a federal employee or contractor who is the victim of terrorism]," 18 U.S.C. 1957(d)

18 U.S.C. 1992 (attacks on railroad and mass transit systems engaged in interstate or foreign commerce)

18 U.S.C. 2151 - 2157 (sabotage)(definitions afford protection for armed forces of the United States and "any associate nation" and for things transported "either within the limits of the United States or upon the high seas or elsewhere," 18 U.S.C. 2151)

18 U.S.C. 2260 (production of sexually explicit depictions of children outside the United States with the intent to import into the United States)

18 U.S.C. 2285 (operation of submersible vessel or semi-submersible vessel without nationality)

Jurisdictional factors: "[t]here is extraterritorial Federal jurisdiction over an offense under this section, including attempt or conspiracy to commit such an offense"

18 U.S.C. 2290
Offenses:

- destruction of vessels or maritime facilities (18 U.S.C. 2291);
- attempting or conspiring to do so (18 U.S.C. 2291); or
- imparting or conveying false information (18 U.S.C. 2292)

Jurisdictional factors:

- victim or offender was a U.S. national;
- U.S. national was aboard victim vessel;
- victim vessel was a U.S. vessel

Attempt/conspiracy

- includes attempts and conspiracies

18 U.S.C. 2332 (killing, attempting or conspiring to kill, or assaulting Americans overseas) (prosecution upon Department of Justice certification of terrorist intent)

18 U.S.C. 2332b

Offenses:

- terrorist acts transcending national boundaries; or
- attempting or conspiring to do so

Jurisdictional factors:

- use of U.S. mail or other facility of United States foreign commerce;
- affects foreign commerce of the United States;
- victim was federal officer or employee or United States government; or
- the offense was committed within the special maritime or territorial jurisdiction of the United States

18 U.S.C. 2339B

Offenses:

- providing material support or resources to designated terrorist organizations by one "subject to the jurisdiction of the United States;" or
- attempting or conspiring to do so

Jurisdictional factors:

- "[t]here is extraterritorial jurisdiction over an offense under this section," 18 U.S.C. 2339B(d)

18 U.S.C. 2339D (receipt of military training from a foreign terrorist organization)

Jurisdictional factors:

- the offender was a United States national;
- the offender was habitual resident of the United States;
- the offender is present in the United States;
- the offense was committed in part in the United States;
- the offense occurred in or affected interstate or foreign commerce; or
- the offender aided or abetted a violation of the section over which extraterritorial jurisdiction exists

18 U.S.C. 2381 (treason) ("within the United States or elsewhere")

18 U.S.C. 2423 (U.S. citizen or resident alien traveling overseas with the intent to commit illicit sexual activity or traveling overseas and thereafter engaging in illicit sexual activity)

18 U.S.C. 2442 (recruitment or use of child soldiers)

Jurisdictional factors:

- the offender was a United States national
- the offender was a stateless person habitually residing in the United States
- the offender is present in the United States
- the offense occurred in part in the United States

18 U.S.C. 3271(overseas overseas transportation of illicit sexual purposes or overseas trafficking in persons – by those employed by or accompanying the United States)

21 U.S.C. 959

Offenses:

- manufacture, distribution or possession of illicit drugs for importation into the United States

Jurisdictional factors:

- "this section is intended to reach acts of manufacture or distribution committed outside the territorial jurisdiction of the United States.... " 21 U.S.C. 959(c)

21 U.S.C. 960A (narco-terrorism)
Jurisdictional factors:

- the offense was a U.S. drug or terrorism offense;
- the offender provided pecuniary value for terrorist offense to injure a U.S. national or damage U.S. property outside the United States;
- the offense was committed in part in the United States and the offender is a U.S. national; or
- the offense occurred in or affected interstate or foreign commerce

46 U.S.C. App. 1903
Offenses:

- manufacture, distribution or possession of controlled substances on various vessels outside United States maritime jurisdiction

Jurisdictional factors:

- the vessel is a "vessel without nationality"; or
- the vessel is of foreign registry or located within foreign territorial waters and the foreign nation has consented to application of the United States law

Federal Crimes Subject to Federal Prosecution When Committed Overseas

Homicide

*7 U.S.C. 2146** (killing federal animal transportation inspectors)
*8 U.S.C. 1324** (death resulting from smuggling aliens into the U.S.)
*15 U.S.C. 1825(a)(2)(C)** (killing those enforcing the Horse Protection Act)
18 U.S.C. 32 (death resulting from destruction of aircraft or their facilities)
Jurisdictional factors:

- aircraft was in the special aircraft jurisdiction of the United States;
- the victim or offender was a United States national; or
- the offender is found in the United States

Attempt/Conspiracy
attempt and conspiracy are included

18 U.S.C. 33 (death resulting from destruction of motor vehicles or their facilities used in United States foreign commerce)

18 U.S.C. 37 (death resulting from violence at international airports)

Jurisdictional factors:

- a victim was a United States national;
- the offender was a United States national; or
- the offender is afterwards found in the United States

18 U.S.C. 38 (death resulting from fraud involving aircraft or space vehicle parts)

Jurisdictional factors:

- the victim or offender was an entity organized under United States law;
- the victim or offender was a United States national; or
- an act in furtherance of the offense was committed in the United States)

18 U.S.C. 43
Offense (where death results):

- travel to disrupt an animal enterprise;
- causing damages of over $10,000 to an animal enterprise; or
- conspiring to cause damages of over $10,000 to an animal enterprise

Jurisdictional factors:

- the offense involved travel in the foreign commerce of the United States; or
- the offense involved use of the mails or other facility in the foreign commerce of the United States

*18 U.S.C. 115(a)(1)(A)** (murder, attempted murder or conspiracy to murder of a family member of a United States officer, employee or judge with intent to impede or retaliate for performance of federal duties)

*18 U.S.C. 115(a)(1)(B)** (murder, attempted murder or conspiracy to murder of a former United States officer, employee or judge or any member of their families in retaliation for performance of federal duties)

18 U.S.C. 175 (death resulting from biological weapons offenses)

Jurisdictional factors:

- a victim was a United States national; or
- the offender was a United States national

18 U.S.C. 175c (variola virus (small pox))
Jurisdictional factors:

- the offender or victim was a United States national;
- the offense occurred in or affected interstate or foreign commerce;
- the offense was committed against U.S. property; or
- the offender aided or abetted the commission of an offense under the section for which there was extraterritorial jurisdiction

18 U.S.C. 229 (death resulting from chemical weapons offenses)
Jurisdictional factors:

- a victim was a United States national;
- the offender was a United States national; or
- committed against United States property

18 U.S.C. 351 (killing a Member of Congress, cabinet officer, or Supreme Court justice)

Attempt/conspiracy

attempt and conspiracy are included

18 U.S.C. 794 (death resulting from disclosing the identify of an American agent to foreign powers)

18 U.S.C. 831
Offenses:

- unlawful possession of nuclear material where the offender causes the death of another; or
- attempting or conspiring to do so

Jurisdictional factors:

- the offense is committed within the special aircraft or special maritime and territorial jurisdiction of the United States;
- a United States national or an American legal entity was the victim of the offense;
- the offender was a United States national or an American legal entity;
- the offender is afterwards found in the United States;
- the offense involved a transfer to or from the United States; or
- the offense was a threat directed against the United States

18 U.S.C.844(d) (death resulting from the unlawful transportation of explosives in United States foreign commerce)

Attempt/conspiracy

attempt and conspiracy are included

*18 U.S.C. 844(f)** (death resulting from bombing federal property)
Attempt/conspiracy
attempt and conspiracy are included
18 U.S.C. 844(i) (death resulting from bombing property used in or used in an activity which affects United States foreign commerce)
Attempt/conspiracy
attempt and conspiracy are included

*18 U.S.C.930** (killing or attempting to kill another during the course of possessing, introducing, or attempting to possess or introduce a firearm or other dangerous weapon in a federal facility)

18 U.S.C. 956 (conspiracy and overt act within the United States to commit murder, kidnaping, maiming or the destruction of certain property overseas)

18 U.S.C.1091 (genocide)\

Jurisdictional factors:

- the offender was a United States national
- the offender is a stateless person habitually residing in the United States
- the offender is present in the United States
- the offense occurred in part in the United States

18 U.S.C.1111 (murder within the special maritime jurisdiction of the United States)

18 U.S.C.1112 (manslaughter within the special maritime jurisdiction of the United States)

18 U.S.C.1113 (attempted murder or manslaughter within the special maritime jurisdiction of the United States)

*18 U.S.C.1114** (murder of a federal employee, including a member of the United States military, or anyone assisting a federal employee or member of the United States military during the performance of (or on account of the performance of) official duties

18 U.S.C.1116 (killing an internationally protected person)

Jurisdictional factors:

- the victim was a United States national;
- the offender was a United States national; or
- the offender is afterwards found in the United States

18 U.S.C.1117 (conspiracy to kill an internationally protected person)

Jurisdictional factors:

- the victim was a United States national;
- the offender was a United States national; or
- the offender is afterwards found in the United States

18 U.S.C.1119 (a United States national killing or attempting to kill a United States national outside the United States)

*18 U.S.C.1120** (murder by a person who has previously escaped from a federal prison)

*18 U.S.C.1121(a)** (killing another who is assisting or because of the other's assistance in a federal criminal investigation or killing (because of official status) a state law enforcement officer assisting in a federal criminal investigation)

18 U.S.C.1201 (kidnaping where death results)

Jurisdictional factors:

- the victim is removed from the United States;
- the offense occurs within the special aircraft or special maritime and territorial jurisdiction of the United States;
- the victim is a federal officer or employee; or
- the victim is an internationally protected person and
  - the victim was a United States national;
  - the offender was a United States national; or
  - the offender is afterwards found in the United States

Attempt/conspiracy

attempt and conspiracy are included

18 U.S.C.1203 (hostage taking where death results)

Jurisdictional factors:

- the victim was a United States national;
- the offender was a United States national; or
- the offender is afterwards found in the United States

Attempt/conspiracy

attempt and conspiracy are included

*18 U.S.C.1347** (defrauding U.S. health care program where death results)

*18 U.S.C.1365** (tampering with consumer products where death results (in the United States))

*18 U.S.C.1503** (killing another to obstruct federal judicial proceedings)

Attempt/conspiracy

attempt is included

18 U.S.C.1512 (tampering with a federal witness or informant where death results)

Jurisdictional factors:

- "[t]here is extraterritorial Federal jurisdiction over an offense under this section," 18 U.S.C.1512(g)

Attempt/conspiracy

attempt is included

18 U.S.C. 1513 (retaliating against a federal witness or informant)

Jurisdictional factors:

- "[t]here is extraterritorial Federal jurisdiction over an offense under this section," 18 U.S.C.1513(d))

Attempt/conspiracy

attempt is included

18 U.S.C. 1652 (murder of an American by an American on the high seas in the name of a foreign state or person)

18 U.S.C. 1751 (killing the President, Vice President, or a senior White House official)

Jurisdictional factors:

- "[t]here is extraterritorial jurisdiction over an offense prohibited by this section," 18 U.S.C.1751(k)

Attempt/conspiracy

attempt and conspiracy are included

18 U.S.C. 1952 (U.S.-foreign travel or use of the mails or of a facility of U.S. foreign commerce in furtherance of a violation of federal arson laws)

18 U.S.C. 1958 (commission of murder for hire in violation of U.S. law where death results)

Jurisdictional factor

- use U.S. foreign travel facilities, or
- use of mails or U.S. foreign commerce facilities

Attempt/conspiracy

- includes conspiracy

18 U.S.C. 1992 (attacks on railroad and mass transit systems engaged in interstate or foreign commerce)

Attempt/conspiracy

- includes attempts and conspiracy

18 U.S.C. 2118 (killing resulting from a robbery or burglary involving controlled substances)

Jurisdictional factors

- offense involved
  - travel in U.S. foreign commerce, or
  - use of a facility in U.S. foreign commerce

Attempt/Conspiracy

attempt and conspiracy prohibitions are included

18 U.S.C. 2119 (death resulting from carjacking)

Jurisdictional factors

- car transported, shipped or received in U.S. foreign commerce in the course of the offense

18 U.S.C.2241, 2245 (aggravated sexual abuse within the special maritime and territorial jurisdiction of the United States where death results)

18 U.S.C.2242, 2245 (sexual abuse within the special maritime and territorial jurisdiction of the United States where death results)

18 U.S.C.2243, 2245 (sexual abuse of a minor or ward within the special maritime and territorial jurisdiction of the United States where death results)

18 U.S.C.2244,2245 (abusive sexual contact within the special maritime and territorial jurisdiction of the United States where death results)

18 U.S.C. 2261A (death resulting from interstate stalking violation involving use of the mails or a facility in U.S. foreign commerce)

Jurisdictional factors

- travel in U.S. maritime jurisdiction; or
- travel in U.S. foreign commerce

18 U.S.C. 2280 (a killing resulting from violence against maritime navigation)

Jurisdictional factors

- aboard a ship of American registry;
- committed by an American national aboard a ship of foreign registry or outside the U.S.;
- victim was an American;
- committed in the territorial waters of another country and the offender is subsequently found in the U.S.; or
- committed in an effort to compel federal action or abstention

18 U.S.C. 2281 (resulting from violence against fixed maritime platforms)

Jurisdictional factors

- aboard a platform on the U.S. continental shelf;
- committed by an American national aboard a platform on the continental shelf of another nation
- victim was an American;
- committed aboard a platform on the continental shelf of another nation and the offender is subsequently found in the U.S.; or
- committed in an effort to compel federal action or abstention

18 U.S.C. 2283 (transportation of explosives, biological, chemical, radioactive or nuclear materials for terrorist purposes on the high seas or aboard a U.S. vessel or in U.S. waters)

18 U.S.C. 2290

Offenses:

- destruction of vessels or maritime facilities (18 U.S.C. 2291); or
- attempting or conspiring to do so (18 U.S.C. 2291)

Jurisdictional factors:

- victim or offender was a U.S. national;
- U.S. national was aboard victim vessel; or
- victim vessel was a U.S. vessel

Attempt/conspiracy

- includes attempts and conspiracies

18 U.S.C. 2332 (killing an American overseas)

Jurisdictional factors

- prosecution only on DoJ certification "to coerce, intimidate, or retaliate against a government or civilian population"

Attempt/conspiracy

- includes attempts and conspiracies

18 U.S.C. 2332a (resulting from use of weapons of mass destruction)

Jurisdictional factors

- victim or offender is American; or
- against federal property

Attempt/conspiracy

- includes attempts and conspiracies

18 U.S.C. 2332f (resulting from bombing of public places, government facilities, public transportation systems or infrastructure facilities)(effective when the terrorist bombing treaty enters into force for the U.S.)
Jurisdictional factors

- victim or offender is American;
- aboard aircraft operated by the U.S.;
- aboard vessel of aircraft of U.S. registry;
- offender is found in the U.S.;
- committed to coerce U.S. action; or
- against federal property

Attempt/conspiracy

includes attempts and conspiracies

18 U.S.C. 2340A (resulting from torture committed outside the U.S.(physical or mental pain inflicted under color of law upon a prisoner))
Jurisdictional factors

- American offender; or
- offender subsequently found within the U.S.

Attempt/conspiracy

includes attempts

18 U.S.C. 2441 (war crimes)
Jurisdictional factors

- victim or offender is an American; or
- victim or offender is a member of U.S. armed forces

18 U.S.C. 3261(offenses committed by members of the United States armed forces or individuals accompanying or employed by the United States armed forces overseas)

*21 U.S.C.461(c)** (murder of federal poultry inspectors during or because of official duties)

*21 U.S.C.675** (murder of federal meat inspectors during or because of official duties)

21 U.S.C.848(e)(1)(B)* (killing a federal or state law enforcement official in furtherance of a federal drug felony)

*21 U.S.C.1041(c)** (murder of an egg inspector during or because of official duties)

*42 U.S.C.2000e-13** (murder, manslaughter or attempted murder or manslaughter of EEOC personnel)

*42 U.S.C.2283** (killing federal nuclear inspectors during or because of official duties)

49 U.S.C. 46502 (air piracy where death results)

49 U.S.C.46506 (murder, manslaughter, or attempted murder or manslaughter within the special aircraft jurisdiction of the United States)

Kidnaping

*18 U.S.C.115(a)(1)(A)** (kidnaping, attempted kidnaping or conspiracy to kidnap a family member of a United States officer, employee or judge with intent to impede or retaliate for performance of federal duties)

*18 U.S.C.115(a)(1)(B)** (kidnaping, attempted kidnaping or conspiracy to kidnap a former United States officer, employee or judge or any member of their families in retaliation for performance of federal duties)

18 U.S.C.351 (kidnaping a Member of Congress, a Supreme Court Justice, or senior executive branch official)

Jurisdictional factors:

- "[t]here is extra territorial jurisdiction over an offense prohibited by this section," 18 U.S.C.351(i)

Attempt/conspiracy

- includes attempts and conspiracies

18 U.S.C. 956 (conspiracy and overt act within the United States to commit murder, kidnaping, maiming or the destruction of certain property overseas)

18 U.S.C. 1091(genocide)

- forcibly transferring children of a national, ethnic, racial or religious group

Jurisdictional factors:

- the offender was a United States national
- the offender is a stateless person habitually residing in the United States
- the offender is present in the United States
- the offense occurred in part in the United States

18 U.S.C.1201 (kidnaping)
Jurisdictional factors:

- the victim is removed from the United States;
- the offense occurs within the special aircraft or special maritime and territorial jurisdiction of the United States;
- the victim is a federal officer or employee; or
- the victim is an internationally protected person and
    - the victim was a United States national;
    - the offender was a United States national; or
    - the offender is afterwards found in the United States

18 U.S.C.1203 (hostage taking)
Jurisdictional factors:

- the victim was a United States national;
- the offender was a United States national; or
- the offender is afterwards found in the United States

Attempt/conspiracy

- includes attempts and conspiracies

18 U.S.C. 1204 (international parental kidnaping detaining a child outside of the United States in violation of parental custody rights)

18 U.S.C. 3261(offenses committed by members of the United States armed forces or individuals accompanying or employed by the United States armed forces overseas)

Assault

7 U.S.C.60* (assault designed to influence administration of federal cotton standards program)

7 U.S.C.87b* (assault designed to influence administration of federal grain standards program)

7 U.S.C.473c-1* (assaults on cotton samplers to influence administration of federal cotton standards program)

7 U.S.C.511i* (assaults designed to influence administration of federal tobacco inspection program)

*7 U.S.C.2146** (assault of United States animal transportation inspectors)

Jurisdictional factors:

- use of U.S. mail or other facility of United States foreign commerce;
- affects foreign commerce of the United States;
- victim was federal officer or employee or United States government; or
- the offense was committed within the special maritime or territorial jurisdiction of the United States

*15 U.S.C.1825(a)(2)(C)** (assaults on those enforcing the Horse Protection Act))

*16 U.S.C.773e** (assaults on officials responsible for enforcing the Northern Pacific Halibut Act)

*16 U.S.C.973c** (assaults on officials responsible for enforcing the South Pacific tuna conversation provisions)

*16 U.S.C.1417** (assaults on officials conducting searches or inspections with respect to the global moratorium on tuna harvesting practices)

*16 U.S.C.1436** (assaults on officials conducting searches or inspections with respect to the marine sanctuaries)

*16 U.S.C.1857, 1859** (assaults on officials conducting searches or inspections with respect to the federal fisheries management and conservation program)

*16 U.S.C.2403, 2408** (assaults on federal officials conducting searches or inspections on vessels subject to the jurisdiction of the United States with respect Antarctic conservation)

*16 U.S.C.2435** (assaults on federal officials conducting searches or inspections on vessels subject to the jurisdiction of the United States in enforcement of the Antarctic Marine Living Resources Convention)

*16 U.S.C.3637** (assaults on federal officials conducting searches or inspections on vessels subject to the jurisdiction of the United States with respect Pacific salmon conservation)

*16 U.S.C.5009** (assaults on federal officials conducting searches or inspections on vessels subject to the jurisdiction of the United States with respect North Pacific anadromous stock conservation)

*16 U.S.C.5505** (assaults on federal officials conducting searches or inspections on vessels subject to the jurisdiction of the United States with respect high seas fishing compliance)

*16 U.S.C.5606** (assaults on federal officials conducting searches or inspections on vessels subject to the jurisdiction of the United States with respect Northwest Atlantic Fisheries Convention compliance)

18 U.S.C.37 (violence at international airports)

Jurisdictional factors:

- a victim was a United States national;
- the offender was a United States national; or
- the offender is afterwards found in the United States

Attempt/conspiracy

- includes attempts and conspiracies

*18 U.S.C.111** (assault on a federal officer or employee)

18 U.S.C.112 (assaulting an internationally protected person)

Jurisdictional factors:

- the victim was a United States national;
- the offender was a United States national; or
- the offender is afterwards found in the United States

18 U.S.C.113 (assault within the special maritime and territorial jurisdiction of the United States)

18 U.S.C.114 (maiming within the special maritime and territorial jurisdiction of the United States)

*18 U.S.C.115(a)(1)(A)** (assaults a family member of a United States officer, employee or judge with intent to impede or retaliate for performance of federal duties)

*18 U.S.C.115(a)(1)(B)** (assaults a former United States officer, employee or judge or any member of their families in retaliation for performance of federal duties)

18 U.S.C.351 (assaulting a Member of Congress, a Supreme Court Justice, or senior executive branch official;

Jurisdictional factor:

"[t]here is extraterritorial jurisdiction over an offense prohibited by this section," 18 U.S.C.351(i)

18 U.S.C. 831

Offenses:

- unlawful use of nuclear material where the offender causes the serious injury to another; or
- attempting or conspiring to do so

Jurisdictional factors:

- the offense is committed within the special aircraft or special maritime and territorial jurisdiction of the United States;
- a United States national or an American legal entity was the victim of the offense;
- the offender was a United States national or an American legal entity;
- the offender is afterwards found in the United States;
- the offense involved a transfer to or from the United States; or
- the offense was a threat directed against the United States

*18 U.S.C.844(f)** (burning or bombing federal property where serious injury results)

18 U.S.C.844(i) (burning or bombing property used in or used in activities affecting United States foreign commerce where serious injury results)

18 U.S.C. 956 (conspiracy and overt act within the United States to commit murder, kidnaping, maiming or the destruction of certain property overseas)

*18 U.S.C. 1091(*genocide)

- assaulting members of a national, ethnic, racial or religious group
- forcibly transferring children of a national, ethnic, racial or religious group

Jurisdictional factors:

- the offender was a United States national
- the offender is a stateless person habitually residing in the United States
- the offender is present in the United States
- the offense occurred in part in the United States

*18 U.S.C.1365** (tampering with consumer products resulting in injury (in the United States))

*18 U.S.C.1501** (assault on a server of federal process)

*18 U.S.C.1502** (assaulting a federal extradition agent)

*18 U.S.C.1503** (assaulting another to obstruct federal judicial proceedings)

18 U.S.C.1512 (tampering with a federal witness or informant through the use of physical force)

Jurisdictional factors:

- "[t]here is extraterritorial Federal jurisdiction over an offense under this section," 18 U.S.C.1512(g)

Attempt/conspiracy

attempt is included

*18 U.S.C.1513**

Offenses (causing physical injury):

- retaliating against a federal witness or informant; or
- attempting to retaliate against a federal witness or informant

Jurisdictional factors:

- "[t]here is extraterritorial Federal jurisdiction over an offense under this section," 18 U.S.C.1513(d))

18 U.S.C. 1655 (assaulting the commander of a vessel is piracy)

18 U.S.C.1751 (assaulting the President, Vice President, or a senior White House official; "[t]here is extraterritorial jurisdiction over an offense prohibited by this section," 18 U.S.C.1751(k))

18 U.S.C.2114 * (assault upon one in possession of the property of the United States)

18 U.S.C. 2191 (cruelty to seamen within the special maritime jurisdiction of the United States)

18 U.S.C. 2194 (shanghaiing sailors for employment within the foreign commerce of the United States)

18 U.S.C.2241 (aggravated sexual abuse within the special maritime and territorial jurisdiction of the United States)

18 U.S.C.2242 (sexual abuse within the special maritime and territorial jurisdiction of the United States)

18 U.S.C.2243 (sexual abuse of a minor or ward within the special maritime and territorial jurisdiction of the United States)

18 U.S.C.2244 (abusive sexual contact within the special maritime and territorial jurisdiction of the United States)

18 U.S.C.2261 (traveling or causing a spouse to travel in foreign commerce of the United States for purposes of domestic violence)

18 U.S.C.2261A (stalking within the special maritime and territorial jurisdiction of the United States)

18 U.S.C.2262 (traveling or causing a spouse to travel in foreign commerce of the United States for purposes violating protective order)

18 U.S.C. 2280

Offenses:

- violence committed against maritime navigation; or
- attempting or conspiracy to commit violence against maritime navigation

Jurisdictional factors:

- the victim was a United States national;
- the offender was a United States national;
- the offender is afterwards found in the United States; or
- the offense was intended to compel action or abstention by the United States

18 U.S.C. 2281
Offenses:

- violence committed against a maritime platform; or
- attempting or conspiracy to commit violence against a maritime platform

Jurisdictional factors:

- the victim was a United States national;
- the offender was a United States national;
- the offender is afterwards found in the United States; or
- the offense was intended to compel action or abstention by the United States

18 U.S.C.2332 (assaulting a United States national outside the United States) (prosecution upon Department of Justice certification of terrorist intent)
18 U.S.C. 2332a
Offenses:

- using a weapon of mass destruction outside the United States resulting physical injury; or
- attempting or conspiring to do so

Jurisdictional factors:

- the victim was a United States national;
- the offender was a United States national; or
- the offense was committed against federal property

18 U.S.C. 2332b
Offenses:

- terrorist assaults transcending national boundaries; or
- attempt or conspiracy

Jurisdictional factors:

- use of U.S. mail or other facility of United States foreign commerce;
- affects foreign commerce of the United States;
- victim was federal officer or employee or United States government; or
- the offense was committed within the special maritime or territorial jurisdiction of the United States

18 U.S.C. 2340A
Offenses:

- torture under color of law outside the United States; or
- attempted torture

Jurisdictional factors:

- the offender was a United States national; or
- the offender is present in the United States

18 U.S.C. 3261(offenses committed by members of the United States armed forces or individuals accompanying or employed by the United States armed forces overseas)

*21 U.S.C.461(c)** (assaulting federal poultry inspectors)

*21 U.S.C.675** (assaulting federal meat inspectors)

*21 U.S.C.1041(c)** (assaulting federal egg inspector)

*30 U.S.C.1461** (assaults on officials conducting searches or inspections with respect to the Deep Seabed Hard Mineral Resources Act)

*42 U.S.C.2000e-13** (assaulting EEOC personnel)

*42 U.S.C.2283** (assaulting federal nuclear inspectors)

46 U.S.C. 11501 (seaman's assault upon officers within the special maritime jurisdiction of the United States)

46 U.S.C. App. 46504 (assaulting officers enforcing regulations of vessels in domestic commerce)

49 U.S.C. 46504 (assaulting a flight crew member within the special aircraft jurisdiction of the United States)

49 U.S.C. 46506 (assaults within the special aircraft jurisdiction of the United States)

Property Destruction

18 U.S.C. 32 (destruction of aircraft or their facilities)
Jurisdictional factors:

- aircraft was in the special aircraft jurisdiction of the United States;
- the victim or offender was a United States national; or
- the offender is found in the United States

Attempt/Conspiracy

attempt and conspiracy are included

18 U.S.C. 33 (destruction of motor vehicles or their facilities used in United States foreign commerce)
18 U.S.C. 37 (violence at international airports)
Jurisdictional factors:

- a victim was a United States national;
- the offender was a United States national; or
- the offender is afterwards found in the United States

18 U.S.C. 43
Offense:

- travel to disrupt an animal enterprise;
- causing damages of over $10,000 to an animal enterprise; or
- conspiring to cause damages of over $10,000 to an animal enterprise

Jurisdictional factors:

- the offense involved travel in the foreign commerce of the United States; or
- the offense involved use of the mails or other facility in the foreign commerce of the United States

18 U.S.C.81 (arson within the special maritime and territorial jurisdiction of the United States)
18 U.S.C. 229 (chemical weapons damage)

Jurisdictional factors:

- a victim was a United States national;
- the offender was a United States national; or
- committed against United States property

18 U.S.C.831 (use nuclear material of damage or destroy)
Jurisdictional factors:

- committed within the special aircraft or special maritime and territorial jurisdiction of the United States
- a United States national or an American legal entity was the victim of the offense;
- the offender was a United States national or an American legal entity;
- the offender is afterwards found in the United States; or
- the offense involved a transfer to or from the United States

*18 U.S.C.844(f)** (burning or bombing federal property)
Attempt/conspiracy

attempt and conspiracy are included

18 U.S.C. 844(i) (burning or bombing property used in or used in an activity which affects United States foreign commerce)
Attempt/conspiracy
attempt and conspiracy are included

18 U.S.C. 956 (conspiracy and overt act within the United States to commit murder, kidnaping, maiming or the destruction of certain property overseas)

18 U.S.C. 1030 (computer abuse involving damage to federal or U.S. financial systems or systems used in the foreign commerce or communications of the United States)

*18 U.S.C.1361** (destruction of federal property)

*18 U.S.C.1362** (destruction of federal communications lines, stations or related property)

18 U.S.C.1363 (destruction of property within the special maritime and territorial jurisdiction of the United States)

18 U.S.C. 1992 (attacks on railroad and mass transit systems engaged in interstate or foreign commerce)

*18 U.S.C.2071** (destruction of federal records)

*18 U.S.C.2153** (war-time destruction of defense materials of the United States or its allies)

*18 U.S.C.2155** (destruction of federal national defense materials)

18 U.S.C.2272 (destruction of a vessel within the maritime jurisdiction of the United States by its owner)

18 U.S.C.2273 (destruction of a vessel within the maritime jurisdiction of the United States by others)

18 U.S.C.2275 (burning or tampering with a vessel within the maritime jurisdiction of the United States)

18 U.S.C.2280 (destruction of maritime navigational facilities)

Jurisdictional factors:

- the offender was a United States national;
- the offender is afterwards found in the United States; or
- the offense was intended to compel action or abstention by the United States

18 U.S.C.2281 (damage to a maritime platform)

Jurisdictional factors:

- the offender was a United States national;
- the offender is afterwards found in the United States; or
- the offense was intended to compel action or abstention by the United States

18 U.S.C. 2290

Offenses:

- destruction of vessels or maritime facilities (18 U.S.C. 2291); or
- attempting or conspiring to do so (18 U.S.C. 2291)

Jurisdictional factors:

- victim or offender was a U.S. national;
- U.S. national was aboard victim vessel;

- victim vessel was a U.S. vessel

18 U.S.C. 2332a (using a weapon of mass destruction)
Jurisdictional factors:

- the victim was a United States national;
- the offender was a United States national; or
- the offense was committed against federal property

18 U.S.C. 2332f (effective upon the terrorist bombing convention entering into force for the U.S.) (bombing public places, government facilities, or public utilities outside the United States)
Jurisdictional factors:

- the victim was a United States national;
- the offender was a United States national;
- the offense was committed against federal property;
- the offender is present in the United States;
- the offense was committed on United States registered vessel or aircraft; or
- the offense was intended to compel action or abstention by the United States

18 U.S.C. 3261(offenses committed by members of the United States armed forces or individuals accompanying or employed by the United States armed forces overseas)

Threats

18 U.S.C.32 (threats to destroy foreign civil aircraft, or aircraft in the special aircraft jurisdiction of the United States, or aircraft or aircraft facilities in the special maritime and territorial jurisdiction of the United States)
18 U.S.C. 112 (threatening internationally protected person)
Jurisdictional factors:

- the victim was a United States national;
- the offender was a United States national; or
- the offender is afterwards found in the United States

*18 U.S.C.115(a)(1)(A)** (threats to assault, murder or kidnap a family member of a United States officer, employee or judge with intent to impede or retaliate for performance of federal duties)

*18 U.S.C.115(a)(1)(B)** (threats to assault, murder or kidnap a former United States officer, employee or judge or any member of their families in retaliation for performance of federal duties)

18 U.S.C.175 (threatening to develop, produce, stockpile, transfer, acquire, retain, or possess biological weapons or delivery systems, misuse of biological weapons; or threatening to assisting a foreign power to do so; "there is extraterritorial Federal jurisdiction over an offense under this section committed by or against a national of the United States," 18 U.S.C.175(a)

18 U.S.C. 229 (threatening to use chemical weapons)

Jurisdictional factors:

- the victim or offender was a United States national; or
- the offense was committed against federal property

18 U.S.C.831 (threaten to use nuclear material of injury or destroy)

Jurisdictional factors:

- committed within the special aircraft or special maritime and territorial jurisdiction of the United States;
- a United States national or an American legal entity was the victim of the offense;
- the offender was a United States national or an American legal entity; or
- the offender is afterwards found in the United States;
- the offense involved a transfer to or from the United States; or
- the offense was a threat directed against the United States

*18 U.S.C. 871** (threatening the President)

18 U.S.C. 875 (transmission of a threat in the foreign commerce of the United States)

18 U.S.C.877 (mailing a threat to kidnap or injure from a foreign country to the United States)

18 U.S.C.878 (threatening to kill, kidnap or assault an internationally protected person)

Jurisdictional factors:

- a victim was a United States national;
- the offender was a United States national; or
- the offender is afterwards found in the United States

*18 U.S.C. 879** (threatening former Presidents)

18 U.S.C.1203 (threaten to kill or injure a hostage outside the United States)

Jurisdictional factors:

- the victim was a United States national;
- the offender was a United States national;
- the offender is afterwards found in the United States; or
- the offense was intended to compel action or abstention by the United States

*18 U.S.C.1503** (obstruction of federal judicial proceedings by threat)

*18 U.S.C.1505** (obstruction of administrative or Congressional proceedings by threat)

18 U.S.C.1512 (threatening a federal witness or informant)

Jurisdictional factors:

- "[t]here is extraterritorial Federal jurisdiction over an offense under this section," 18 U.S.C.1512(g)

18 U.S.C. 1513 (threatening to retaliate against a federal witness or informant)

Jurisdictional factors:

- "[t]here is extraterritorial Federal jurisdiction over an offense under this section," 18 U.S.C.1513(d))

18 U.S.C. 1992 (threatening a terrorist attack on mass transit)

Jurisdictional factor

- the victim was mass transit in or affecting U.S. foreign commerce, or
- the offender travels or communicates across a state line

18 U.S.C.2280 (threats of violence against maritime navigation)
Jurisdictional factors:

- the victim was a United States national;
- the offender was a United States national;
- the offender is afterwards found in the United States; or
- the offense was intended to compel action or abstention by the United States

18 U.S.C.2281 (threatens injury or destruction aboard a fixed maritime platform)
Jurisdictional factors:

- the victim was a United States national;
- the offender was a United States national;
- the offender is afterwards found in the United States; or
- the offense was intended to compel action or abstention by the United States

18 U.S.C. 2290
Offenses:

- destruction of vessels or maritime facilities (18 U.S.C. 2291); or
- attempting or conspiring to do so (18 U.S.C. 2291)

Jurisdictional factors:

- victim or offender was a U.S. national;
- U.S. national was aboard victim vessel;
- victim vessel was a U.S. vessel

18 U.S.C. 2332a (threatening to use a weapon of mass destruction)
Jurisdictional factors:

- the victim was a United States national;
- the offender was a United States national; or
- the offense was committed against federal property

18 U.S.C. 2332f (effective upon the terrorist bombing convention entering into force for the U.S.) (threatening to bomb public places, government facilities, or public utilities outside the United States)

Jurisdictional factors:

- the victim was a United States national;
- the offender was a United States national;
- the offense was committed against federal property;
- the offender is present in the United States;
- the offense was committed on United States registered vessel or aircraft; or
- the offense was intended to compel action or abstention by the United States

49 U.S.C.46507 (threats or scares concerning air piracy or bombing aircraft in the special aircraft jurisdiction of the United States)

False Statements

*8 U.S.C.1160(b)(7)(A)** (falsification of an application for immigration status)

*15 U.S.C.158** (false or fraudulent statements by China Trade Act corporate personnel)

*15 U.S.C.645** (false statements associated with the Small Business Administration)

*15 U.S.C.714m** (false statements associated with the Commodity Credit Corporation)

*16 U.S.C.831t** (false statements associated with TVA)

*18 U.S.C.152 ** (false statements in bankruptcy)

*18 U.S.C.287** (false or fraudulent claims against the United States)

*18 U.S.C.288** (false claims for postal losses)

*18 U.S.C.289** (false claims for pensions)

18 U.S.C.541 (entry of goods falsely classified)

18 U.S.C.542 (entry of goods by means of false statements)

18 U.S.C.550 (false claim for refund of duties)

*18 U.S.C.1001** (false statement on a matter within the jurisdiction of a federal agency)

*18 U.S.C.1002** (possession of false papers to defraud the United States)

*18 U.S.C.1003** (fraudulent claims against the United States)

*18 U.S.C.1007** (false statements in an FDIC transaction)

*18 U.S.C.1011** (false statements in federal land bank mortgage transactions)

*18 U.S.C.1014** (false statements in loan or credit applications in which the United States has an interest)

18 U.S.C.1015 (false statements concerning naturalization, citizenship or alien registry)

18 U.S.C.1019 (false certification by consular officer)

*18 U.S.C.1020** (false statements concerning highway projects)

18 U.S.C.1022 (false certification concerning material for the military)

*18 U.S.C.1027** (false statements to facilitate a theft concerning ERISA)

18 U.S.C. 1039 (obtaining confidential communications information by fraud)

18 U.S.C.1542 (false statement in application for a passport)

18 U.S.C.1546 (fraud in connection with visas, permits and other documents)

*18 U.S.C.1621** (perjury)

*18 U.S.C.1622** (subornation of perjury)

*22 U.S.C.1980** (false statement to obtain compensation for loss of commercial fishing vessel or gear)

22 U.S.C.4221 (perjury or false swearing before American diplomatic personnel)

22 U.S.C.4222 (presentation of forged documents to United States foreign service personnel)

*42 U.S.C.408** (false statement in old age claims)

*42 U.S.C.1320a-7b** (false statements concerning Medicare)

Theft

*7 U.S.C.2024(b)** (food stamp fraud)

*15 U.S.C.645** (embezzlement or fraud associated with the Small Business Administration)

*15 U.S.C.714m** (embezzlement or fraud associated with the Commodity Credit Corporation)

*16 U.S.C.831t** (theft associated with TVA)

18 U.S.C.371 (conspiracy to defraud the United States)

*18 U.S.C.641** (theft of federal property)

*18 U.S.C.645** (theft by federal court officers)

*18 U.S.C.648** (theft of federal property by custodians)

*18 U.S.C.656** (embezzlement from a federally insured bank)

*18 U.S.C.657** (embezzlement from a federally insured credit union)

*18 U.S.C.658** (theft of property mortgaged or pledged to federal farm credit agencies)

18 U.S.C.661 (theft within the special maritime and territorial jurisdiction of the United States)

18 U.S.C.662 (receipt of stolen property within the special maritime and territorial jurisdiction of the United States)

18 U.S.C.831 (theft of nuclear materials)

Jurisdictional factors:

- within the special aircraft or special maritime and territorial jurisdiction of the United States;
- the victim was a United States national or an American legal entity;
- the offender was a United States national or an American legal entity;
- the offender is afterwards found in the United States; or
- the offense involved a transfer to or from the United States

18 U.S.C.1025 (theft by false pretenses or fraud within the special maritime and territorial jurisdiction of the United States)

*18 U.S.C.793-798** (espionage)

*18 U.S.C.1010** (fraud to secure loan or credit advance from HUD)

*18 U.S.C.1013** (fraud in connection with farm loan bonds or credit bank debentures)

*18 U.S.C.1023** (fraud in connection with deliveries for military services)

*18 U.S.C.1024** (receipt of stolen military property)

*18 U.S.C.1026** (fraudulently securing the cancellation of farm debt to the United States)

*18 U.S.C.1030** (fraud in connection with computers)

*18 U.S.C.1031** (major fraud against the United States)

*18 U.S.C.1506** (theft or alteration of court records)

*18 U.S.C.1707** (theft of postal service property)

*18 U.S.C.1711** (theft of postal funds)

*18 U.S.C.2071** (destruction of United States records)

*18 U.S.C.2112** (robbery of the personal property of the United States)

*18 U.S.C.2115** (robbery of a post office)

18 U.S.C. 3261(offenses committed by members of the United States armed forces or individuals accompanying or employed by the United States armed forces overseas)

*20 U.S.C.1097** (fraud in connection with financial aid to students)

*22 U.S.C.4217** (embezzlement by American diplomatic personnel)

*25 U.S.C.450d** (theft involving the Indian Self-Determination and Education Assistance Act)

*38 U.S.C.787** (fraud concerning veterans' life insurance)

*42 U.S.C.1307** (social security fraud)

*42 U.S.C.1383a** (fraud in connection with supplemental security income for the blind, aged and disabled)

*42 U.S.C.1713** (fraud in connection in connection with claims for injuries overseas associated with contracts for the United States)

*42 U.S.C.1760(g)** (theft in connection with the school lunch program)

*42 U.S.C.1761(o)** (fraud in connection with summer food programs)

*42 U.S.C.3220** (fraud and theft concerning public works and economic development)

*42 U.S.C.3795** (fraud or theft of funds associated with the Office of Justice Programs)

*45 U.S.C.359** (fraud in connection with railroad unemployment insurance)

*46 U.S.C. App. 1276** (fraud in connection with federal ship mortgage insurance)

Counterfeiting

18 U.S.C.470-474 (counterfeiting United States obligations outside the United States)

*18 U.S.C.484** (connecting parts of different notes of the United States)

*18 U.S.C.486** (uttering United States coins of gold, silver or other metal)

*18 U.S.C.487** (making or possessing counterfeit dies for United States coins)

*18 U.S.C.490** (counterfeiting minor United States coins)

*18 U.S.C.491** (counterfeiting tokens or paper used as money of the United States)

*18 U.S.C.493** (counterfeiting bonds and obligations of certain federal lending agencies)

*18 U.S.C.494** (forging contractors bonds, bids or public records in order to defraud the United States)

*18 U.S.C.495** (forging contracts, deeds or powers of attorney in order to defraud the United States)

*18 U.S.C.496** (counterfeiting United States customs entry certificates)

*18 U.S.C.497** (counterfeiting United States letters patent)

*18 U.S.C.498** (counterfeiting United States military or naval discharge certificates)

*18 U.S.C.499** (counterfeiting United States military, naval or official passes)

18 U.S.C.500 *(counterfeiting United States postal money orders)

*18 U.S.C.501** (counterfeiting United States postal stamps)

*18 U.S.C.503** (counterfeiting postmarking stamps)

*18 U.S.C.505** (counterfeiting federal judicial documents)

*18 U.S.C.506** (counterfeiting federal agency seals)

*18 U.S.C.507** (forging or counterfeiting ships papers)

*18 U.S.C.508** (forging or counterfeiting government transportation requests)

*18 U.S.C.509** (possession of plates to counterfeiting government transportation requests)

*18 U.S.C.510** (forging endorsements on Treasury checks)

*18 U.S.C.513** (counterfeiting state securities)

*18 U.S.C.514** (transmitting, transporting, or sending a fictitious U.S. financial instrument in the foreign commerce of the United States)

Piggyback Statutes

18 U.S.C.2 (principals)

18 U.S.C.3 (accessories after the fact)

18 U.S.C.4 (misprision)

18 U.S.C.371 (conspiracy)

18 U.S.C.924(c), (j) (using or carrying a firearm during the course of a federal crime of violence or drug trafficking crime)

18 U.S.C. 1952 (Travel Act)

18 U.S.C. 1956-1957 (money laundering)

18 U.S.C. 1959 (violence in aid of racketeering)

18 U.S.C. 1961-1965 (RICO)

21 U.S.C. 846 (conspiracy or attempt to violate the Controlled Substances Act)

21 U.S.C. 963 (conspiracy or attempt to violate the Controlled Substances Import and Export Act)

Model Penal Code

§1.03 Territorial Applicability

(1) Except as otherwise provided in this Section, a person may be convicted under the law of this State of an offense committed by his own conduct or the conduct of another for which he is legally accountable if:

- (a) either the conduct that is an element of the offense or the result that is such an element occurs within this State; or
- (b) conduct occurring outside the State is sufficient under the law of this State to constitute an attempt to commit an offense within the State; or
- (c) conduct occurring outside the State is sufficient under the law of this State to constitute a conspiracy to commit an offense within the state and an overt act in furtherance of such conspiracy occurs within the state; or
- (d) conduct occurring within the State establishes complicity in the commission of, or an attempt, solicitation or conspiracy to commit , an offense in another jurisdiction that also is an offense under the law of this State; or
- (e) the offense consists of the omission to perform a legal duty imposed by the law of this State with respect to domicile, residence or a relationship to a person, thing or transaction in the State; or
- (f) the offense is based on a statute of this State that expressly prohibits conduct outside the State, when the conduct bears a reasonable relation to a legitimate interest of this State and the actor knows or should know that his conduct is likely to affect that interest.

(2) Subsection (1)(a) does not apply when either causing a specified result or a purpose to cause or danger of causing such a result is an element of an offense and the result occurs or is designed or likely to occur only in another jurisdiction where the conduct charged would not constitute an offense, unless a legislative purpose plainly appears to declare the conduct criminal regardless of the place of the result.

(3) Subsection (1)(a) does not apply when causing a particular result is an element of an offense and the result is caused by conduct occurring outside the State that would not constitute an offense if the result had

occurred there, unless the actor purposely or knowingly caused the result within the State.

(4) When the offense is homicide, either the death of the victim or the bodily impact causing death constitutes a result within the meaning of Subsection (a)(1), and if the body of a homicide victim is found within the State, it is presumed that such result occurred within the State.

(5) This State includes the land and water and the air space above such land and water with respect to which the State has legislative jurisdiction.

Restatement of the Law Third: Foreign Relations Law of the United States

§401. Categories of Jurisdiction

Under international law, a state is subject to limitations on

(a) jurisdiction to prescribe, i.e., to make its law applicable to the activities, relations, or status of persons, or the interests of persons in things, whether by legislation, by executive act or order, by administrative rule or regulation, or by determination of a court;

(b) jurisdiction to adjudicate, i.e., to subject persons or things to the process of its courts or administrative tribunals, whether in civil or in criminal proceedings, whether or not the state is a party to the proceedings;

(c) jurisdiction to enforce, i.e., to induce or compel compliance or to punish noncompliance with its laws or regulations, whether through the courts or by use of executive, administrative, police, or other nonjudicial action.

§402. Bases of Jurisdiction to Prescribe

Subject to §403, a state has jurisdiction to prescribe law with respect to

(1)

(a) conduct that, wholly or in substantial part, takes place within its territory;

(b) the status of persons, or interests in things, present within its territory;

(c) conduct outside its territory that has or is intended to have substantial effect within its territory;

(2) the activities, interests, status, or relations of its nationals outside as well as within its territory; and

(3) certain conduct outside its territory by persons not its nationals that is directed against the security of the state or against a limited class of other state interests.

§403. Limitations on Jurisdiction to Prescribe

(1) Even when one of the bases for jurisdiction under §402 is present, a state may not exercise jurisdiction to prescribe law with respect to a person or activity having connections with another state when the exercise of such jurisdiction is unreasonable.

(2) Whether exercise of jurisdiction over a person or activity is unreasonable is determined by evaluating all relevant factors, including, where appropriate:

(a) the link of the activity to the territory of the regulating state, i.e., the extent to which the activity takes place within the territory, or has substantial, direct, and foreseeable effect upon or in the territory;

(b) the connections, such as nationality, residence, or economic activity, between the regulating state and the person principally responsible for the activity to be regulated, or between that state and those whom the regulation is designed to protect;

(c) the character of the activity to be regulated, the importance of regulation to the regulating state, the extent to which other states regulate such activities, and the degree to which the desirability of such regulation is generally accepted;

(d) the existence of justified expectations that might be protected or hurt by the regulation;

(e) the importance of the regulation to the international political, legal, or economic system;

(f) the extent to which the regulation is consistent with the traditions of the international system;

(g) the extent to which another state may have an interest in regulating the activity; and

(h) the likelihood of conflict with regulation by another state.

(3) When it would not be unreasonable for each of two states to exercise jurisdiction over a person or activity, but the prescriptions by the two states are in conflict, each state has an obligation to evaluate its own as well as the other state's interest in exercising jurisdiction, in light of all the relevant factors, Subsection (2); a state should defer to the other state if that state's interest is clearly greater.

§404. Universal Jurisdiction to Define and Punish Certain Offenses

A state has jurisdiction to define and prescribe punishment for certain Offenses recognized by the community of nations as of universal concern, such as piracy, slave trade, attacks on or hijacking of aircraft, genocide, war crimes, and perhaps certain acts of terrorism, even where none of the jurisdiction indicated in §402 is present.

§421. Jurisdiction to Adjudicate

(1) A state may exercise jurisdiction through its courts to adjudicate with respect to a person or thing if the relationship of the state to the person or thing is such as to make the exercise of jurisdiction reasonable.
(2) In general, a state's exercise of jurisdiction to adjudicate with respect to a person or thing is reasonable if, at the time jurisdiction is asserted:
   (a) the person or thing is present in the territory of the state, other than transitorily;
   (b) the person, if a natural person, is domiciled in the state;
   (c) the person, if a natural person, is resident in the state;
   (d) the person, if a natural person, is a national of the state;
   (e) the person, if a corporation or comparable juridical person, is organized pursuant to the law of the state;
   (f) a ship, aircraft, or other vehicle to which the adjudication relates is registered under the laws of the state;
   (g) the person, whether natural or juridical, has consented to the exercise of jurisdiction;
   (h) the person, whether natural or juridical, regularly carries on business in the state;
   (i) the person, whether natural or juridical, had carried on activity in the state, but only in respect to such activity;

(j) the person, whether natural or juridical, had carried on outside the state an activity having a substantial, direct, and foreseeable effect within the state, but only in respect to such activity; or
(k) the thing that is the subject of adjudication is owned, possessed, or used in the state, but only in respect to a claim reasonably connected with that thing.

(3) A defense of lack of jurisdiction is generally waived by any appearance by or on behalf of a person or thing (whether as plaintiff, defendant, or third party), if the appearance is for a purpose that does not include a challenge to the exercise of jurisdiction.

§431. Jurisdiction to Enforce

(1) A state may employ judicial or nonjudicial measures to induce or compel compliance or punish noncompliance with its laws or regulations, provided it has jurisdiction to prescribe in accordance with §§402 and 403.
(2) Enforcement measures must be reasonably related to the laws or regulations to which they are directed; punishment for noncompliance must be preceded by an appropriate determination of violation and must be proportional to the gravity of the violation.
(3) A state may employ enforcement measures against a person located outside the territory
    (a) if the person is given notice of the claims or charges against him that is reasonable in the circumstances;
    (b) if the person is given an opportunity to be heard, ordinarily in advance of enforcement, whether in person or by counsel or other representative; and
    (c) when enforcement is through the courts, if the state has jurisdiction to adjudicate.

18 U.S.C. 7. Special Maritime and Territorial Jurisdiction of the Untied States (Text)

The term "special maritime and territorial jurisdiction of the United States", as used in this title, includes:

(1) The high seas, any other waters within the admiralty and maritime jurisdiction of the United States and out of the jurisdiction of any particular State, and any vessel belonging in whole or in part to the United States or any citizen thereof, or to any corporation created by or under the laws of the United States, or of any State, Territory, District, or possession thereof, when such vessel is within the admiralty and maritime jurisdiction of the United States and out of the jurisdiction of any particular State.
(2) Any vessel registered, licensed, or enrolled under the laws of the United States, and being on a voyage upon the waters of any of the Great Lakes, or any of the waters connecting them, or upon the Saint Lawrence River where the same constitutes the International Boundary Line.
(3) Any lands reserved or acquired for the use of the United States, and under the exclusive or concurrent jurisdiction thereof, or any place purchased or otherwise acquired by the United States by consent of the legislature of the State in which the same shall be, for the erection of a fort, magazine, arsenal, dockyard, or other needful building.
(4) Any island, rock, or key containing deposits of guano, which may, at the discretion of the President, be considered as appertaining to the United States.
(5) Any aircraft belonging in whole or in part to the United States, or any citizen thereof, or to any corporation created by or under the laws of the United States, or any State, Territory, District, or possession thereof, while such aircraft is in flight over the high seas, or over any other waters within the admiralty and maritime jurisdiction of the United States and out of the jurisdiction of any particular State.
(6) Any vehicle used or designed for flight or navigation in space and on the registry of the United States pursuant to the Treaty on Principles Governing the Activities of States in the Exploration and Use of Outer Space, Including the Moon and Other Celestial Bodies and the Convention on Registration of Objects Launched into Outer Space, while that vehicle is in flight, which is from the moment when all external doors are closed on Earth following embarkation until the moment when one such door is opened on Earth for disembarkation or in the case of a forced landing, until the competent authorities take over the responsibility for the vehicle and for persons and property aboard.

(7) Any place outside the jurisdiction of any nation with respect to an offense by or against a national of the United States.
(8) To the extent permitted by international law, any foreign vessel during a voyage having a scheduled departure from or arrival in the United States with respect to an offense committed by or against a national of the United States.
(9) With respect to Offenses committed by or against a national of the United States as that term is used in section 101 of the Immigration and Nationality Act—
  (A) the premises of United States diplomatic, consular, military or other United States Government missions or entities in foreign States, including the buildings, parts of buildings, and land appurtenant or ancillary thereto or used for purposes of those missions or entities, irrespective of ownership; and
  (B) residences in foreign States and the land appurtenant or ancillary thereto, irrespective of ownership, used for purposes of those missions or entities or used by United States personnel assigned to those missions or entities.

Nothing in this paragraph shall be deemed to supersede any treaty or international agreement with which this paragraph conflicts. This paragraph does not apply with respect to an offense committed by a person described in section 3261(a) of this title.

18 U.S.C. 3261. Military Extraterritorial Jurisdiction (Text)

(a) Whoever engages in conduct outside the United States that would constitute an offense punishable by imprisonment for more than 1 year if the conduct had been engaged in within the special maritime and territorial jurisdiction of the United States –
  (1) while employed by or accompanying the Armed Forces outside the United States; or
  (2) while a member of the Armed Forces subject to chapter 47 of title 10 (the Uniform Code of Military Justice), shall be punished as provided for that offense.
(b) No prosecution may be commenced against a person under this section if a foreign government, in accordance with jurisdiction recognized by the United States, has prosecuted or is prosecuting such

person for the conduct constituting such offense, except upon the approval of the Attorney General or the Deputy Attorney General (or a person acting in either such capacity), which function of approval may not be delegated.

(c) Nothing in this chapter may be construed to deprive a court-martial, military commission, provost court, or other military tribunal of concurrent jurisdiction with respect to offenders or offenses that by statute or by the law of war may be tried by a court-martial, military commission, provost court, or other military tribunal.

(d) No prosecution may be commenced against a member of the Armed Forces subject to chapter 47 of title 10 (the Uniform Code of Military Justice) under this section unless –

(1) such member ceases to be subject to such chapter; or

(2) an indictment or information charges that the member committed the offense with one or more other defendants, at least one of whom is not subject to such chapter.

BIBLIOGRAPHY

Books and Articles

[1] Abbell, Extradition to and from the United States (2010)

[2] _____, Obtaining Evidence Abroad in Criminal Cases (2010)

[3] Abramovsky, *Extraterritorial Jurisdiction: The United States Unwarranted Attempt to Alter International Law in United States v. Yunis*, 15 Yale Journal of International Law 121 (1990)

[4] Abramovsky & Edelstein, *Time for Final Action on 18 U.S.C. 3292*, 21 Michigan Journal of International Law 941 (2000)

[5] American Law Institute, Restatement of the Law Third: The Foreign Relations Law of the United States (1987)

[6] Bassiouni, International Extradition: United States Law and Practice (5th ed. 2007)

[7] Blakesley, *A Conceptual Framework for Extradition and Jurisdiction Over Extraterritorial Crimes*, 1984 Utah Law Review 685

[8] Blakesley & Stigall, *The Myopia of U.S. v. Martinelli: Extraterritorial Jurisdiction in the 21st Century*, 39 George Washington International Law Review 1 (2007)

[9] Born, *Reappraisal of the Extraterritorial Reach of United States Law*, 24 Law & Policy In International Business 1 (1992)

[10] Bradley, *Universal Jurisdiction and United States Law*, 2001 University Of Chicago Legal Forum 323

[11] Brilmayer, *The Extraterritorial Application of American Law: A Methodological and Constitutional Appraisal*, 50 Law & Contemporary Problems 11 (1987)

[12] Brilmayer & Norchi, *Federal Extraterritoriality and Fifth Amendment Due Process*, 105 Harvard Law Review 1217 (1992)

[13] Cabranes, *Our Imperial Criminal Procedure: Problems in the Extraterritorial Application of U.S. Constitutional Law*, 118 Yale Law Journal 1660 (2009)

[14] Carey, *Should American Courts Listen to What Foreign Courts Hear? The Confrontation and Hearsay Problems of Prior Testimony Taken Abroad in Criminal Proceedings*, 29 American Journal Of Criminal Law 29 (2001)

[15] Colangelo, *Constitutional Limits on Extraterritorial Jurisdiction: Terrorism and the Intersection of National and International Law*, 48 Harvard International Law Journal 121 (2007)

[16] _____, *Unified Approach to Extraterritoriality*, 97 Virginia Law Review 1019 (2011)

[17] Condon, *Extraterritorial Interrogation: The Porous Border Between Torture and U.S. Criminal Trials*, 60 Rutgers Law Review 647 (2008)

[18] Clopton, *Bowman Lives: The Extraterritorial Application of U.S. Criminal Law After Morrison v. National Australia Bank*, 67 New York University Annual Survey of American Law 137 (2011)

[19] Garrett, *Globalized Corporate Prosecutions*, 97 Virginia Law Review 1775 (2011)

[20] George, *Extraterritorial Application of Penal Legislation*, 64 Michigan Law Review 609 (1966)

[21] Gibney, *The Extraterritorial Application of United States Law: The Perversion of Democratic Governance, the Reversal of Institutional Roles, and the Imperative of Establishing Normative Principles*, 19 Boston College International & Comparative Law Review 297 (1996)

[22] Gordon, *United States Extraterritorial Subject Matter Jurisdiction in Securities Fraud Litigation*, 10 Florida Journal of International Law 487 (1996)

[23] Grandman, *New Imperialism: The Extraterritorial Application of United States Law*, 14 International Lawyer 257 (1980)

[24] Griffin, *Foreign Governmental Reactions to United States Assertions of Extraterritorial Jurisdiction*, 6 George Mason Law Review 505 (1998)

[25] Harvard Research in International Law, *Jurisdiction With Respect to Crime*, 72 American Journal of International Law (Supp.) 485 (1935)

[26] Kontorovich, *Beyond the Article I Horizon: Congress's Enumerated Powers and Universal Jurisdiction Over Drug Crimes*, 93 Minnesota Law Review 1191 (2009)

[27] ____, *The "Define and Punish" Clause and the Limits of Universal Jurisdiction*, 103 Northwestern University Law Review 149 (2009)

[28] Meyer, *Dual Illegality and Geoambiguous Law: A New Rule for Extraterritorial Application of U.S. Law*, 95 Minnesota Law Review 110 (2010)

[29] Paust, *Non-Extraterritoriality of "Special Territorial Jurisdiction" of the United States: Forgotten History and the Errors of Erdos*, 24 Yale Journal Of International Law 305 (1999)

[30] Perkins, *The Territorial Principle in Criminal Law*, 22 Hastings Law Journal 1155 (1971)

[31] Podgor, *Globalization and the Federal Prosecution of White Collar Crime*, 34 American Criminal Law Review 325 (1997)

[32] ___, *International Computer Fraud: A Paradigm for Limiting National Jurisdiction,* 35 University Of California Davis Law Review 267 (2002)

[33] Podgor & Filler, *International Criminal Jurisdiction in the Twenty-First Century: Rediscovering United States v. Bowman*, 44 San Diego Law Review 585 (2007)

[34] Randall, *Universal Jurisdiction Under International Law*, 66 Texas Law Review 785 (1988)

[35] Richardson, *Due Process for the Global Crime Age: A Proposal*, 41 Cornell International Law Journal 347 (2008)

[36] Smith, *In re Forfeiture Proceedings and Extraterritorial Jurisdiction*, 45 International & Comparative Law Quarterly 902 (1996)

[37] Snow, *The Investigation and Prosecution of White Collar Crime: International Challenges and the Legal Tools Available to Address Them*, 11 William & Mary Bill Of Rights Journal 20-9 (2002)

[38] Tuerkheimer, Globalization of United States Law Enforcement: Does the Constitution Come Along? 39 Houston Law Review 307 (2002)

[39] United States Congress, *Legislative Initiatives to Curb Domestic and International Terrorism; Hearings Before the Subcomm. on Security and Terrorism of the Senate Comm. on the Judiciary*, 98th Cong., 2d Sess. (1984)

[40] ___, *Bills to Authorize Prosecution of Terrorists and Others Who Attack United States Government Employees and Citizens Abroad: Hearing Before the Subcomm. on Security and Terrorism of the Senate Comm. on the Judiciary*, 99th Cong., 1st Sess. (1985)

[41] ___, *Extraterritorial Jurisdiction Over Terrorists Acts Abroad: Hearings Before Subcomm. on Crime of House Comm. on Judiciary*, 101st Cong., 1st Sess. (1989)

[42] van der Vyver, Prosecuting Offenses Against the Law of Nations in the United States, 20 Emory International Law Review 473 (2006)

[43] Warner, Challenges to International Law Enforcement Cooperation for the United States in the Middle East and North Africa: Extradition and Its Alternatives, 50 Villanova Law Review 479 (2005)

[44] Watson, Offenders Abroad: The Case for Nationality-Based Criminal Jurisdiction, 17 Yale Journal Of International Law 41 (1992)

[45] ___, The Passive Personality Principle, 28 Texas International Law Journal 1 (1993)

[46] Weisburd, *Due Process Limits on Federal Extraterritorial Legislation?* 35 Columbia Journal Of Transnational Law 379 (1997)

[47] Yost & Anderson, The Military Extraterritorial Jurisdiction Act of 2000: Closing the Gap, 33 Connecticut Law Review 446 (2001)

[48] Zabel, *Extraterritoriality*, 26 Harvard International Law Journal 569 (1985)

Notes and Comments

[1] *Constructing the State Extraterritorially: Jurisdictional Discourse, the National Interests, and Transnational Norms*, 103 Harvard Law Review 1273 (1990)

[2] *Defining and Punishing Abroad: Constitutional Limits on the Extraterritorial Reach of the Offenses Clause*, 48 Duke Law Journal 1305 (1999)

[3] *The Five Bases of Extraterritorial Jurisdiction and the Failure of the Presumption Against Extraterritoriality*, 33 Hastings International & Comparative Law Review 177 (1997)

[4] *The Fourth Amendment and Remote Searches: Balancing the Protection of "The People" With the Remote Investigation of Internet Crimes*, 19 Notre Dame Journal of Law, Ethics & Public Policy 355 (2005)

[5] *From a Pakistani Station House to the Federal Court House: A Confession's Uncertain Journey in the U.S.-Led War on Terror*, 12 Cardozo Journal Of International And Comparative Law 297 (2004)
[6] *Love's Labour's Lost: Michael Lewis Clark's Constitutional Challenge of 18 U.S.C. 2423(C),* 43 American Criminal Law Review 1241 (2006)
[7] *Predictability and Comity: Toward Common Principles of Extraterritorial Jurisdiction*, 98 Harvard Law Review 1310 (1985)
[8] *Protecting National Interests: The Legal Status of Extraterritorial Law Enforcement by the Military*, 41 Duke Law Journal 867 (1992)
[9] *The Protective Principle of Extraterritorial Jurisdiction: A Brief History and an Application of the Principle to Espionage as an Illustration of Current United States Practice*, 6 Boston University International Law Journal 337 (1988)
[10] *United States v. Jura: Fifth Amendment Due Process and Stateless Vessels on the High Seas*, 73 Boston University Law Review 477 (1993)
[11] *United States v. Passaro: Exercising Extraterritorial Jurisdiction Over Non-Defense Department Government Contractors Committing Crimes Overseas Under the Special Maritime and Territorial Jurisdiction of the Untied States*, 58 Catholic University Law Review 1143 (2009)
[12] *United States v. Yunis: The D.C. Circuit's Dubious Approval of United States Long-arm Jurisdiction Over Extraterritorial Crime*, 87 Northwestern University Law Review 697 (1993)

End Notes

[1] The general and almost universal rule is that the character of an act as lawful or unlawful must be determined wholly by the law of the country where the act is done," *American Banana Co v. United Fruit Co.*, 213 U.S. 347, 356 (1909).

[2] In the parlance of international law, the term "states" ordinarily refers to nation states. Here and hereinafter, however, the term refers to the several states of the United States, unless otherwise indicated or apparent from the context found within a quotation.

[3] U.S. Const. Art. I, §8, cls. 10, 3; Art. VI, cl. 2,

[4] U.S. Const. Art.I, §8, cl. 10; *see generally, The Offences Clause After* Sosa v. Alvarez-Machain, 118 HARVARD LAW REV. 2378 (2005); Stephens, *Federalism and Foreign Affairs: Congress's Power to "Define and Punish ... Offenses Against the Law of Nations,"* 42 WILLIAM & MARY LAW REVIEW 447 (2000).

[5] U.S. Const. Art. I, §8, cl.3.

[6] U.S. Const. Art. I, §8, cl.18.

[7] *United States v. Ibarguen-Mosquera,* 634 F.3d 1370, 1378-379 (11th Cir. 2011)(upholding application of the Drug Trafficking Vessel Interdiction Act (18 U.S.C. 2285) under the piracy, high seas, and law of nations clause); *United States v. Motos-Luchi*, 627 F.3d 1, 3 (1st Cir. 2010)(noting Congress's invocation of the clause to enact the Maritime Drug Law

Enforcement Act(46 U.S.C. 70501 et seq.)); *United States v. Shi*, 525 F.3d 709, 721-22(9th Cir. 2008)(noting Congress's authority under the clause and under the necessary and proper clause (U.S. Const. Art. I, §8, cl.18)(with respect to legislation carrying into execution the President's treaty powers) to enact 18 U.S.C. 2280 (relating to maritime violence)).

[8] *United States v. Flores*, 289 U.S. 137, 159 (1933)(Flores, an American seaman, was convicted of murdering another American aboard an American ship moored 250 miles up the Congo River (well within the territorial jurisdiction of the then Belgian Congo) under the federal statute proscribing murder committed within the special maritime jurisdiction of the United States).

[9] U.S. Const. Art. I, §8, cl.3.

[10] See e.g., *Heart of Atlanta Motel v. United States*, 379 U.S. 241, 255-58 (1964); *Perez v. United States*, 402 U.S. 146, 156-57 (1971); *Gonzales v. Raich*, 545 U.S. 1, 5 (2005).

[11] *California Bankers Ass'n v. Shultz*, 416 U.S. 21, 46 (1974)("the plenary authority of Congress over both interstate and foreign commerce is not open to dispute"); *United States v. 12,200-Ft. Reels of Film*, 413 U.S. 123, 125 (1973)("The Constitution gives Congress broad, comprehensive powers 'to regulate Commerce with foreign Nations'").

[12] *United States v. Yunis*, 681 F.Supp. 896, 907 n.24 (D.D.C. 1988)("Rather than relying on Congress's direct authority under Art. I Section 8 to define and punish offenses against the law of nations, the government contends that Congress has authority to regulate global air commerce under the commerce clause. U.S. Const. art. I, § 8, c. 3. The government's arguments based on the commerce clause are unpersuasive. Certainly Congress has plenary power to regulate the flow of commerce within the boundaries of United States territory. But it is not empowered to regulate foreign commerce which has no connection to the United States. Unlike the states, foreign nations have never submitted to the sovereignty of the United States government nor ceded their regulatory powers to the United States"). See also, Colangelo, *Constitutional Limits on Extraterritorial Jurisdiction: Terrorism and the Intersection of National and International Law*, 48 HARVARD INTERNATIONAL LAW JOURNAL 121, 149-50 (2007)(emphasis in the original) ("Furthermore, as a matter of original intent, the idea that the Foreign Commerce Clause might license Congress with the broad ability to extend U.S. laws extraterritorially into the jurisdictions of other nations would have been anathema to the founders given their driving belief in the sovereign equality of states and its accompanying rigid concept of territoriality – which to borrow yet again from Chief Justice Marshall held that 'no [state] can rightfully impose a rule on another[,] [each] legislates for itself, but its legislation can operate on itself alone.' Recall the reason why Congress was allowed to legislate extraterritorially over piracy absent a U.S. connection even though the act technically occurred within another state's territory: the conduct was prohibited as a matter of *the law of nations*, not of U.S. law, and thus the United States was not imposing its *own* rule on other nations, but merely enforcing (on their behalf) a universal norm when it prosecuted pirates. No such analysis applies to extraterritorial projections of Congress' Foreign Commerce Clause power").

[13] *United States v. Clark*, 435 F.3d 1100, 1103 (9th Cir. 2006)("Instead of slavishly marching down the path of grafting the interstate commerce framework onto foreign commerce, we step back and take a global, commonsense approach to the circumstances presented here: The illicit sexual conduct reached by the state expressly includes commercial sex acts performed by a U.S. citizen on foreign soil. This conduct might be immoral and criminal, but it is also commercial. Where, as in this appeal, the defendant travels in foreign commerce to a foreign country and offers to pay a child to engage in sex acts, his conduct falls under the broad umbrella of foreign commerce and consequently within congressional authority under the Foreign Commerce Clause").

[14] *Id.* at 1109-110 ("At the outset, we highlight that §2423(c) contemplates two types of 'illicit sexual conduct': noncommercial and commercial. Clark's conduct falls squarely under the second prong of the definition, which criminalizes 'any commercial sex act ... with a person under 18 years of age.' §2423(f)(2). In view of this factual posture, we abide by the rule that

courts have a 'strong duty to avoid constitutional issues that need not be resolved in order to determine the rights of the parties to the case under consideration, and limit our holding to §2423(c)'s regulation of commercial sex acts").

[15] *United States v. Weingarten*, 632 F.3d 60, 70-71 (2d Cir. 2011)(emphasis in the original)("We note, finally, that our determination that §2423(b) does not extend to travel occurring wholly between foreign nations and without any territorial nexus to the United States appropriately avoids the necessity of addressing whether such an exercise of congressional power would comport with the Constitution.... We note, in addition, that the issue of statutory construction that this case represents would be substantially different if §2423(b) prohibited travel for the purpose of engaging in the defined sexual acts where such travel *affects* foreign commerce. Section 2423(b), however, prohibits travel *in* foreign commerce, and Count Three which involved simply a flight from Belgium, where the defendant resided, to Israel, his new home, did not constitute such travel").

[16] *United States v. Pendleton*, 658 F.3d 299, 308, 311 & n.7 (3d Cir. 2011)(here and elsewhere internal citations are generally omitted)("[B]ecause the jurisdictional element in §2423(c) ['travels in foreign commerce'] has an 'express connection' to the channels of foreign commerce, we hold that its is a valid exercise of Congress's power under the Foreign Commerce Clause. N.7 Having found that the statute is constitutional under the first prong of *Lopez*, we need not address Pendleton's contention that §2423(f)(1) does not survive *Morrison's* stringent 'substantial effects' test ... ").

[17] U.S.Const. Art.I, §8, cl.18 ("The Congress shall have Power ... To make all Laws which shall be necessary and proper for carrying into Execution the foregoing Powers, and all other Powers vested by this Constitution in the Government of the United States, or in any Department or Officer thereof").

[18] See e.g., "The President shall be Commander in Chief of the Army and Navy of the United States, and of the Militia of the several States.... He shall have Power, by and with the Advice and Consent of the Senate, to make Treaties, provided two thirds of the Senators present concur; and he shall nominate, and by and with the Advice and Consent of the Senate, shall appoint Ambassadors.... He ... shall receive Ambassadors and other public Ministers; [and] he shall take Care that the Laws be faithfully executed.... " U.S. Const. Art.II, §§2, 3.

"The Congress shall have Power To lay and collect Taxes, Duties, Imposts and Excises ... ; To establish an uniform Rule of Naturalization ... ; To declare War, grant Letters of Marque and Reprisal, and make Rules concerning Captures on Land and Water; To raise and support Armies ... ; To provide and maintain a Navy; To make Rules for the Government and Regulation of the land and naval Forces; ... [and] To make all Laws which shall be necessary and proper for carrying into Execution the foregoing Powers, and all other Powers vested by this Constitution in the Government of the United States, or in any Department or Officer thereof." U.S. Const. Art.I, §8, cls.1, 4, 11-14, 18.

[19] *United States v. Curtiss-Wright Corp.*, 299 U.S. 304, 315-18 (1936); *Ex parte Quirin*, 317 U.S. 1, 28-9 (1942); *Parker v. Levy*, 417 U.S. 733, 756-57 (1974); *United States v. Belfast*, 611 F.3d 783, 805 (11th Cir. 2010) ("Congressional power to pass those laws necessary and property to effectuate the enumerated powers of the Constitution is nowhere broader and more important than in the realm of foreign relations.... It follows generally that if a treaty is valid there can be no dispute about the validity of a statute passed under Article I, Section 8, as a necessary and proper means to execute the powers of the Government").

Some judicial authorities have suggested that in the area of foreign affairs the Constitution's establishment of the federal government as a sovereign entity vested it with authority, defined by standards recognized by the law of nations, beyond or in lieu of its constitutionally enumerated powers. *United States v. Rodriguez*, 182 F.Supp. 479, 490- 91 (S.D.Cal. 1960), aff'd sub nom., *Rocha* v. *United States*, 288 F.2d 545 (9th Cir. 1961)("The powers of the government and the Congress in regard to sovereignty are broader than the powers possessed in relation to internal matters, *United States v. Curtiss-Wright Export*

Corp., 1936, 299 U.S. 304: 'The broad statement that the federal government can exercise no powers except those specifically enumerated in the Constitution, and such implied powers as are necessary and proper to carry into effect the enumerated powers, is categorically true only in respect to our internal affairs.' Id., 299 U.S. at page 315.... 'It results that the investment of the federal government with the powers of external sovereignty did not depend upon the affirmative grants of the Constitution. Id. 299 U.S. at page 318.' ... To put it in more general terms, the concept of essential sovereignty of a free nation clearly requires the existence and recognition of an inherent power in the state to protect itself from destruction. This power exists in the United States government absent express provision in the Constitution and arises from the very nature of the government which was created by the Constitution").

[20] *Curtiss-Wright* suggests that the same can be said of any sovereign-based legislative authority, 299 U.S. at 318 ("Neither the Constitution nor the laws passed in pursuance of it have any force in foreign territory unless in respect of our own citizens; and operations of the nation in such territory must be governed by treaties, international understandings and compacts, and the principles of international law.... [T]he court recognized, and in each of the cases cited [involving the exercise of the sovereign power of the United States] found, the warrant for its conclusions not in the provisions of the Constitution, but in the law of nations").

[21] E.g., *United States v. Belfast*, 611 F.3d 783, 804 (11th Cir. 2010)(quoting *United States v. Comstock,* 130 S.Ct 1949, 1956 (2010) and upholding Congress's authority under the necessary and proper clause to carrying into execution the President's treaty power by enacting the Torture Act (18 U.S.C. 2340-2340B))("Thus, in determining whether the Necessary and Proper Clause grants Congress the legislative authority to enact a particular federal statute, we look to see whether the statute constitutes a means that is rationally related to the implementation of a constitutionally enumerated power"); *Toth v. Quarles*, 350 U.S. 11, 13-4 (1955) (court martial trial of a civilian for crimes he allegedly committed in Korea while in the military exceeded the authority granted Congress by Art.I, §8, cl.14 and Art.III, §2); *Kinsella v. Singleton*, 361 U.S. 234, 247-48 (1960)(holding that Congressional authority under Art.I, §8, cl.14 to make rules and regulations governing the land and naval forces did not include authority for the court martial trial of civilian dependents for offenses committed overseas); *consider*, Lowenfeld, *U.S. Law Enforcement Abroad: The Constitution and International Law*, 83 AMERICAN JOURNAL OF INTERNATIONAL LAW 880, 891-92 (1989) (asserting that the creation of subject matter and personal jurisdiction over an alien defendant for an offense committed overseas and not otherwise connected to the United States by forcibly bringing him into the United States is "not clearly within any constitution grant of power to Congress, and in particular, ... does not, as written, come within the power to define and punish offenses against the law of nations").

[22] The due process clause of the Fourteenth Amendment limits the legislative authority of the states.

[23] *Cf., Skiriotes v. Florida*, 313 U.S. 69, 77 (1941)("[W]e see no reason why the State of Florida may not likewise govern the conduct of its citizens upon the high seas with respect to matters in which the State has a legitimate interest and where there is no conflict with acts of Congress"); *American Insurance Ass'n v. Garamendi*, 539 U.S. 396, 413 (2003)("There is, of course, no question that at some point an exercise of state power that touches on foreign relations must yield to the National Government's policy, given the concern for uniformity in this country's dealing with foreign nations that animated the Constitution's allocation of the foreign relations power to the National Government in the first place").

[24] "No person shall... be deprived of life, liberty, or property, without due process of law.... " U.S. Const. Amend.V. " [N]or shall any State deprive any person of life, liberty, or property, without due process of law... " U.S. Const. Amend.XIV, §1.

[25] See e.g., *United States v. Yousef*, 327 F.3d 56, 86 (2d Cir. 2003); *United States v. Thomas*, 893 F.2d 1066, 1068 (9th Cir. 1990); *United States v. Quemener*, 789 F.2d 145, 156 (2d Cir.

1986); *United States v. Henriquez*, 731 F.2d 131, 134-35 n.4, 5(2d Cir. 1984); *United States v. Pinto-Mejia*, 720 F.2d 248, 259 (2d Cir. 1983); *United States v. Howard- Arias*, 679 F.2d 363, 371 (4th Cir. 1982).

[26] *United States v. Verdugo-Urquidez*, 494 U.S. 259, 278 (1990) (Kennedy, J., concurring) ("I do not mean to imply, and the Court has not decided, that persons in the position of the respondent have no constitutional protection. The United States is prosecuting a foreign national in a court established under Article III, and all of the trial proceedings are governed by the Constitution. All would agree, for instance that the dictates of the Due Process Clause of the Fifth Amendment protect the defendant").

[27] "The global view... of the Constitution is also contrary to this Court's decisions in the *Insular Cases*, which held that not every constitutional provision applies to governmental activity even where the United States has sovereign power... [I]t is not open to us in light of the *Insular Cases* to endorse the view that every constitutional provision applies wherever the United States Government exercises its power. Indeed, we have rejected the claim that aliens are entitled to Fifth Amendment rights outside the sovereign territory of the United States." *United States v. Verdugo-Urquidez*, 494 U.S. at 268-71.

[28] *Morrison v. National Australia Bank Ltd.*, 130 S.Ct. 2869, 2877 (2010)(internal citations omitted)("It is a longstanding principle of American law that legislation of Congress, unless a contrary intent appears, is meant to apply only within the territorial jurisdiction of the United States. This principle represents a canon of construction, or a presumption about a statute's meaning, rather than a limit upon Congress's power to legislate"); *EEOC v. Arabian American Oil Co.*, 499 U.S. at 248 ("Both parties concede, as they must that Congress has the authority to enforce its laws beyond the territorial boundaries of the United States. Whether Congress has in fact exercised that authority in this case is a matter of statutory construction").

[29] *United States v. Medjuck*, 156 F.3d 916, 918 (9th Cir. 1998)("to satisfy the strictures of due process, the Government [must] demonstrate that there exists a sufficient nexus between the conduct condemned and the United States such that the application of the statute [to the overseas conduct of an alien defendant] would not be arbitrary or fundamentally unfair to the defendant"), citing, *United States v. Davis*, 905 F.2d at 248-49; see also, *United States v. al Kassar*, 660 F.3d 108, 118 (2d Cir. 2011)("In order to apply extraterritorially a federal criminal statute to a defendant consistently with due process, there must be a sufficient nexus between the defendant and the United States, so that such application would not be arbitrary or fundamentally unfair"); *United State v. Perlaza*, 439 F.3d 1149, 1160-161 (9th Cir. 2006); *United States v. Moreno-Morillo*, 334 F.3d 819, 828 (9th Cir. 2003); *United States v. Klimavicius-Viloria*, 144 F.3d 1249, 1256 (9th Cir. 1998); *United States v. Greer*, 956 F.Supp. 531, 534-36 (D.Vt. 1997); *United States v. Aikens*, 946 F.2d 608, 613-14 (9th Cir. 1990); *United States v. Robinson*, 843 F.2d 1, 5-6 (1st Cir. 1988); *United States v. Peterson*, 812 F.2d 486, 493 (9th Cir. 1987); *United States v. Gonzalez*, 776 F.2d 931, 938-41 (11th Cir. 1985).

These "subject matter" or "legislative" jurisdiction due process questions have arisen more often from attempts to impose civil liability or regulatory obligations, particularly at the state level, *see e.g., Gerling Global Reinsurance Corp. v. Gallagher*, 267 F.3d 1228, 1234-238 (11th Cir. 2001)(due process precludes application of Florida's Holocaust Victims Insurance Act to insurance policies issued outside the state, to persons outside the state, and covering individuals outside the state); *see also, Gerling Global Reinsurance Corp. v. Low*, 240 F.3d 739, 753 (9th Cir. 2001); *Watson v. Employers Liability Assurance Corp.*, 348 U.S. 66, 70-1 (1954)("because the policy was bought, issued and delivered outside of Louisiana, Employers invokes the due process principle that a state is without power to exercise 'extra territorial jurisdiction' that is, to regulate and control activities wholly beyond its boundaries").

[30] *United States v. Davis*, 905 F.2d 245, 249 n.2 (9th Cir. 1990) ("International law principles may be useful as a rough guide of whether a sufficient nexus exists between the defendant and

the United States so that application of the statute in question would not violate due process. However, danger exists that emphasis on international law principles will cause us to lose sight of the ultimate question: would application of the statute to the defendant be arbitrary or fundamentally unfair?"); *United States v. Ibarguen-Mosquera*, 634 F.3d 1370, 1379 (11th Cir. 2011); *cf., United States v. Caicedo*, 47 F.3d 370, 372-73 (9th Cir. 1995).

[31] *United Sates v. Clark*, 435 F.3d 1100, 1108 (9th Cir. 2006)("Although Clark's citizenship alone is sufficient to satisfy due process concerns, his U.S. investments, ongoing receipt of federal retirement benefits and use of U.S. military flights also underscore his multiple and continuing ties with this country"); *United States v. Zakharov*, 468 F.3d 1171, 1177 (9th Cir. 2006)("Nexus is a constitutional requirement analogous to 'minimum contacts' in personal jurisdiction analysis"); *United States v. Klimavicius-Viloria*, 144 F.3d at 1257 (citing *World-Wide Volkswagen Corp. v. Woodson*, 444 U.S. 286, 297 (1980)); *United States v. Aikens*, 946 F.2d 608, 613-14 (9th Cir. 1990); *United States v. Robinson*, 843 F.2d 1, 5-6 (1st Cir. 1988); *United States v. Peterson*, 812 F.2d 486, 493 (9th Cir. 1987); *United States v. Gonzalez*, 776 F.2d 931, 938-41 (11th Cir. 1985).

[32] Brilmayer & Norchi, *Federal Extraterritoriality and Fifth Amendment Due Process*, 105 HARVARD LAW REVIEW 1217 (1992); Weisburd, *Due Process Limits on Federal Extraterritorial Legislation?* 35 COLUMBIA JOURNAL OF TRANSNATIONAL LAW 379 (1997); *Due Process and True Conflicts: The Constitutional Limits on Extraterritorial Federal Legislation and the Cuban Liberty and Democratic Solidarity (Libertad) Act of 1996*, 46 CATHOLIC UNIVERSITY LAW REVIEW 907 (1997); Colangelo, *Constitutional Limits on Extraterritorial Jurisdiction: Terrorism and the Intersection of National and International Law*, 48 HARVARD INTERNATIONAL LAW JOURNAL 121 (2007).

[33] *United States v. Ibarguen-Mosquera*, 634 F.3d 1370, 1378-379 (11th Cir. 2011)(internal citations omitted)("In determining whether an extraterritorial law comports with due process, appellate courts often consult international law principles.... In the past we have held that [these] ... principles have no applicability in connection with stateless vessels because such vessels are international pariahs that have no internationally recognized right to navigate freely on the high seas. Indeed, the law places no restrictions upon a nation's right to subject stateless vessels to its jurisdiction"); *United States v. Suerte*, 291 F.3d 366, 375 (5th Cir. 2002)("[T]o the extent the Due Process Clause may constrain the MDLEA's extraterritorial reach, that clause does not impose a nexus requirement, in that Congress has acted pursuant to the Piracies and Felonies Clause"); *United States v. Perez-Oviedo*, 281 F.3d 400, 403 (3d Cir. 2002)(internal citations omitted)("[N]o due process violation occurs in an extraterritorial prosecution under MDLEA when there is no nexus between the defendant's conduct and the United States. Since drug trafficking is condemned universally by lawabiding nations ... there is no reason for us to conclude that it is 'fundamentally unfair' for Congress to provide for the punishment of a person apprehended with narcotics on the high seas ... Perez-Oviedo's state of facts presents an even stronger case for concluding that no due process violation occurred. The Panamanian government expressly consented to the application of the MDLEA ... Such consent from the flag nation eliminates a concern that the application of the MDLEA may be arbitrary or fundamentally unfair"); *United States v. Cardales*, 168 F.3d 548, 553 (1st Cir. 1999) ("[D]ue process does not require the government to prove a nexus between a defendant's criminal conduct and the United States in a prosecution under the MDLEA when the flag nation has consented to the application of United States law to the defendants").

[34] "The rule that ignorance of the law will not excuse is deep in our law, as is the principle that of all the powers of local government, the police power is one of the least limitable. On the other hand, due process places some limits on its exercise. Ingrained in our concept of due process is the requirement of notice.... As Holmes wrote in the Common Law, 'A law which punished conduct which would not be blameworthy in the average member of the community would be too severe for that community to bear.' Its severity lies in the absence of an opportunity either to avoid the consequences of the law or to defend any prosecution

brought under it. Where [as here] a person did not know of the duty to register and where there was no proof of the probability of such knowledge, he may not be convicted consistently with due process. Were it otherwise, the evil would be as great as it is when the law is written in print too fine to read or *in a language foreign to the community*." *Lambert v. California*, 355 U.S. 225, 228-30(1957)(emphasis added); *accord, United States v. Vasarajs*, 908 F.2d 443, 448-49 (9th Cir. 1990); *Griffin v. Wisconsin*, 483 U.S. 868, 875 n.3 (1987); *United States v. Shi*, 525 F.3d 709, 722 (9th Cir. 2008)("The Due Process Clause requires that a defendant prosecuted in the United States should reasonably anticipate being haled into court in this country").

[35] *United States v. Belfast*, 611 F.3d 783, 809 (11th Cir. 2010)("The Supreme Court made clear long ago that an absent United States citizen is nonetheless personally bound to take notice of this laws of the United States that are applicable to him and to obey them"); *United States v. Bin Laden*, 92 F.Supp.2d 189, 218 (S.D.N.Y. 2000)("Odeh argues that application of Sections 844(f), (h), and (n); 924(c); 930(c); and 2155 to the extraterritorial conduct he is alleged to have engaged in would violate his due process right to a fair warning.... The Government responds that while Odeh may not have known that breadth of the statutory framework that would serve as the basis for the charges against him ... there is no room for him to suggest that he has suddenly learned that mass murder was illegal in the United States or anywhere else.... The Government also argues that Odeh cannot be surprised to learn that his conduct was criminal under the laws of every civilized nation, and thus he has no right to complain about the particular forum in which he is brought to trial. We likewise find this argument persuasive"); *United States v. Saac*, 632 F.3d 1203, 1210 (11th Cir. 2011)("In as much as the trafficking of narcotics is condemned universally by law-abiding nations, we see no reason to conclude that it is fundamentally unfair for Congress to provide for the punishment of persons apprehended with narcotics on the high seas"); *United States v. Campbell*, 798 F.Supp.2d 293, 306-307 (D.D.C. 2011)("Whether the test for due process in such a circumstance requires a 'sufficient nexus' to the United States, commonly understood as real effects or consequences accruing in this country, or prosecution that is neither arbitrary or capricious has split the circuits. One line of cases reasons that '[i]n order to apply extraterritorially a federal criminal statute to a defendant consistently with due process, there must be a sufficient nexus between the defendant and the United States so that such application would not be arbitrary or fundamentally unfair.' ... In contrast, several circuits require only that extraterritorial prosecution be neither arbitrary nor fundamentally unfair, and are not concerned with whether a sufficient nexus exists").

[36] *Consider, e.g., United States v. Henriquez*, 731 F.2d 131, 134 n.5 (2d Cir. 1984)("It is also argued that 21 U.S.C. §955a(a) as applied [possession of marijuana with intent to distribute by Colombian nationals aboard a non-American vessel in international waters] violates the notice requirement of the due process clause of the Fifth Amendment. *See Lambert v. California*.... The argument is based not only on the claim that the statute is unprecedented in international law and the proposition that marijuana trafficking itself is not universally condemned, but also on the alleged vagueness of the definition of 'vessel without nationality' in 21 U.S.C. §955b(d) [upon which federal jurisdiction was based]. On this point, however, we agree with the Eleventh Circuit ... that the term 'vessel without nationality' clearly encompasses vessels not operating under the authority of any sovereign nation"); *United States v. Alvarez-Mena*, 765 F.2d 1259, 1267 n.11 (5th Cir. 1985) ("[n]evertheless, we observe that we are not faced with a situation where the interests of the United States are not even arguably potentially implicated. The present case is not remotely comparable to, for example, the case of an unregistered small ship owned and manned by Tanzanians sailing from that nation to Kenya on which a crew member carries a pound of marihuana to give to a relative for his personal consumption in the latter country")(example offered in discussion of presumption of Congressional intent).

[37] *EEOC v. Arabian American Oil Co.*, 499 U.S. 244, 248 (1991); *Foley Brothers v. Filardo*, 336 U.S. 281, 284-85 (1949)("The question before us is not the power of Congress to extend the

eight hour law to work performed in foreign countries. Petitioners concede that such power exists. The question is rather whether Congress intended to make the law applicable to such work"); *United States v. Yousef*, 327 F.3d 56, 86 (2d. Cir. 2003)("It is beyond doubt that, as a general proposition, Congress has the authority to enforce its laws beyond the territorial boundaries of the United States"); *United States v. Martinez*, 599 F.Supp.2d 784, 796-97 (W.D.Tex. 2009).

[38] "It is a 'long-standing principle of American law that legislation of Congress, unless a contrary intent appears, is meant to apply only within the territorial jurisdiction of the United States,'" *Morrison v. National Australia*, 130 S.Ct. 2869, 2877 (2010), quoting, *EEOC. v. Arabian American Oil Co.*, 499 U.S. at 248 (1991); see also, *Argentine Republic v. Amerada Hess Shipping*, 488 U.S. 428, 440 (1989); *Sale v. Haitian Centers Council, Inc.*, 509 U.S. 155, 173 (1993); *Smith v. United States*, 507 U.S. 197, 203 (1993); *Small v. United States*, 544 U.S. 385, 388-89 (2005); *cf., The Antelope*, 23 U.S. 30, 53-4 (10 Wheat. 66, 123) (1825)("The courts of no country will execute the penal laws of another"). The principle has a corollary, the so-called revenue rule, which precludes judicial enforcement of a foreign tax laws, *Pasquantino v. United States*, 544 U.S. 349, 360-61 (2005). The rule, however, does not preclude enforcement of a federal criminal statute which proscribes defrauding a foreign country of its tax revenues, *id.* at 354- 55 ("the common-law revenue rule, rather than barring any recognition of foreign revenue law, simply allow[s] courts to refuse to enforce the tax judgments of foreign nations, and therefore [does] not preclude the Government from prosecuting ... ").

[39] See e.g., *American Banana Co. v. United Fruit Co.*, 213 U.S. at 355-56, "It is obvious that, however stated, the plaintiff's case depends on several rather startling propositions. In the first place the acts causing the damage were done so far as appears, outside the jurisdiction of the United States and within that of other states. It is surprising to hear it argued that they were governed by the act of Congress.

"No doubt in regions subject to no sovereign, like the high seas, or to no law that civilized countries would recognize as adequate, such countries may treat some relations between their citizens as governed by their own law, and keep to some extent the old notion of personal sovereignty alive. They go further at times and declare that they will punish any one, subject or not, who shall do certain things, if they can catch him, as in the case of pirates on the high seas. In cases immediately affecting national interests they may go further still and may make, and, if they get the chance, execute similar threat as to acts done within another recognized jurisdiction. An illustration from our statutes is found with regard to criminal correspondence with foreign governments.... "

[40] 260 U.S. 94, 97-98102 (1922)("We have in this case a question of statutory construction. The necessary *locus*, when not specifically defined, depends upon the purpose of Congress as evinced by the description and nature of the crime and upon the territorial limitations upon the power and jurisdiction of a government to punish crime under the law of nations. Crimes against private individuals or their property, like assaults, murder, burglary, larceny, robbery, arson, embezzlement and frauds of all kinds, which affect the peace and good order of the community, must of course be committed within the territorial jurisdiction of the government where it may properly exercise it. If punishment of them is to be extended to include those committed outside the strict territorial jurisdiction, it is natural for Congress to say so in the statute, and failure to do so will negate the purpose of Congress in this regard. We have an example of this in the attempted application of the prohibitions of the Anti-Trust Law to acts done by citizens of the United States against other such citizens in a foreign country. *American Banana Co.* v. *United Fruit Co.*, 213 U.S. 347. That was a civil case, but as the statute is criminal as well as civil, it presents an analogy.

"But the same rule of interpretation should not be applied to criminal statutes which are, as a class, not logically dependent on their locality for the government's jurisdiction, but are enacted because of the right of the government to defend itself against obstruction, or fraud wherever perpetrated, especially if committed by its own citizens, officers or agents. Some such offenses can only be committed within the territorial jurisdiction of the Government because of the local acts required to constitute them. Others are such that to limit their *locus* to the strictly territorial jurisdiction would be greatly to curtail the scope and usefulness of the statute and leave open a large immunity for frauds as easily committed by citizens on the high seas and in foreign countries as at home. In such cases, Congress has not thought it necessary to make specific provision in the law that the *locus* shall include the high seas and foreign countries, but allows it to be inferred from the nature of the offense.... Clearly it is no offense to the dignity or right of sovereignty of Brazil [– where the fraud of which the United States government was the target occurred –] to hold [these American defendants] for this crime against the government to which they owe allegiance"). See also, *United States v. Delgado-Garcia*, 374 F.3d 1337, 1344-350 (D.C. Cir. 2004); *United States v. Villanueva*, 408 F.3d 193, 197-98 (5th Cir. 2005); *United States v. Lopez-Vanegas*, 493 F.3d 1305, 1311-312 (11th Cir. 2007).

41 130 S.Ct. 2869, 2881 (2010)("The results of judicial-speculation-made-law – divining what Congress would have wanted if it had thought of the situation before the court – demonstrate the wisdom of the presumption in all cases, preserving a stable background against which Congress can legislate with predictable results").

42 *United States v. al Kassar*, 660 F.3d 108, 118 (2d Cir. 2011)(some internal citations omitted)("The presumption that ordinary acts of Congress do not apply extraterritorially does not apply to criminal statutes. *United States v. Bowman*"); *United State v. Leija-Sanchez*, 602 F.3d 797, 799 (7th Cir. 2010)("Whether or not ... post-1922 decisions are in tension with *Bowman*, we must apply *Bowman* until the Justices themselves overrule it"); *United States v. Campbell*, 798 F.Supp.2d 293, 303 (D.D.C 2011)(footnote 3 of the opinion in brackets) ("The Supreme Court has not limited or overruled *Bowman*. Despite the emphasis of *Morrison* that the presumption against extraterritoriality applies 'in all cases,' 130 S.Ct. at 2881, recent Supreme Court jurisprudence has developed with nary a mention of *Bowman* and has predominately involved civil statutes. [Many courts since Morrison have continued to find that *Bowman* presents an exception to, or overcomes, the presumption against extraterritoriality, or have otherwise found no tension between the two cases. See e.g., United States v. Weingarten, 632 F.3d 60, 65-67 (2d Cir. 2011)(acknowledging *Morrison* and then noting that, per *Bowman*, Congress is presumed to have intended the extraterritorial reach of criminal statutes where the nature of the crime is not dependent on the location of the acts and limiting the statute to U.S. territory would significantly diminish its effectiveness); *United States v. Belfast*, 611 F.3d 783, 811, 813-14 (11th Cir. 2010)(citing *Morrison* for the proposition that the presumption against extraterritoriality may only be overcome by clear expression of congressional intent, which may be inferred per *Bowman* from the nature of the offense and whether denying extraterritoriality would limit the scope and usefulness of the statute) . . .. Other courts have noted that *Bowman* has not been overruled or limited by subsequent case law. See *United States v. Leija-Sanchez.... United States v. Finch*, Crim. No. 10-333, 2010 U.S. Dist. LEXIS 104496, at *12 (D. Haw. Sept. 30, 2010)('Morrison neither explicitly nor implicitly overrules Bowman, which counsels courts to examine statutes with an eye toward whether Congress intended to protect the Government from crimes wherever perpetrated')].... No doubt courts do and should presume criminal laws to have only domestic application absent affirmative evidence to the contrary ... but *Morrison*'s insistence on a textual foundation in the statutory language is not found in *Bowman*, which relied on the Supreme Court's perception of an implied congressional intent of extraterritoriality for a specific grouping of crimes against the U.S. government"); see also, Clopton, Bowman Lives: The Extraterritorial Application of U.S. Criminal Law After Morrison v. National Australia Bank, 67 NEW YORK UNIVERSITY ANNUAL SURVEY OF AMERICAN LAW 137 (2011).

43 "It has been a maxim of statutory construction since the decision in *Murray v. The Charming Betsy*, 2 Cranch [6 U.S.] 64, 118 (1804), that an act of Congress ought never to be construed to violate the law of nations, if any other possible construction remains," *Weinberger v.*

Rossi, 456 U.S. 25, 32 (1982); *The Apollon*, 22 U.S. (9 Wheat.) 362, 370-71 (1824)("It cannot be presumed, that Congress would voluntarily justify ... a clear violation of the law of nations").

[44] E.g., *The Apollon*, 22 U.S. (9 Wheat.) at 370 ("The laws of no nation can justly extend beyond its own territories, *except so far as regards its own citizens*")(emphasis added); *American Banana Co. v. United Fruit Co.*, 213 U.S. at 355-6 ("No doubt in regions subject to no sovereign, like the high seas, or to no law that civilized countries would recognize as adequate, such countries may treat some relations between their citizens as governed by their own law, and keep to some extent the old notion of personal sovereignty alive.... And the notion that English statutes bind British subjects everywhere has found expression in modern times and has had some startling applications"); *United States v. Bowman*, 260 U.S. at 102 ("Section 41 of the Judicial Code provides that 'the trial of all offenses committed on the high seas, or elsewhere out of the jurisdiction of any particular State or district, shall be in the district where the offender is found, or into which he is first brought.' The three defendants who were found in New York were citizens of the United States and were certainly subject to such laws as it might pass to protect itself and its property. Clearly it is no offense to the dignity or right of sovereignty of Brazil to hold them for this crime against the government to which they owe allegiance. The other defendant is a subject of Great Britain. He has never been apprehended, and it will be time enough to consider what, if any, jurisdiction the District Court below has to punish him when he is brought to trial"); *United States v. Columba-Colella*, 604 F.2d 356, 360 (5th Cir. 1979) ("Congress [is] not competent to attach criminal sanctions to the murder of an American by a foreign national in a foreign country ... ").

[45] E.g., *United States v. Vasquez-Velasco*, 15 F.3d 833, 839-41 (9th Cir. 1994)(prosecution under 18 U.S.C. 1959 for the murder of two American tourists in Mexico by Mexican nationals acting under the mistaken belief that the Americans were DEA agents came within the principle recognized in international law as permitting the exercise of extraterritorial jurisdiction in the name of a nation's security); *United States v. Yunis*, 924 F.2d 1086, 1091 (D.C.Cir. 1991); *United States v. Felix-Gutierrez*, 940 F.2d 1200, 1205-206 (9th Cir. 1991)(murder of an American agent overseas); *United States v. Benitez*, 741 F.2d 1312, 1316-317 (11th Cir. 1986); see also, *United States v. Bin Laden*, 92 F.Supp.2d 189, 194-95 (S.D.N.Y.2000) (concluding that *Bowman* applies regardless of the nationality of the offender).

[46] "Yunis seeks to portray international law as a self-executing code that trumps domestic law whenever the two conflict. That effort misconceives the role of judges as appliers of international law and as participants in the federal system. Our duty is to enforce the Constitution, laws, and treaties of the United States, not to conform the law of the land to norms of customary international law," *United States v. Yunis*, 924 F.2d 1086, 1091 (D.C.Cir. 1991); *United States v. Yousef*, 327 F.3d 56, 86 (2d Cir. 2003)("In determining whether Congress intended a federal statute to apply to overseas conduct, an act of Congress ought never to be construed to violate the law of nations if any other possible construction remains. Nonetheless, in fashioning the reach of our criminal law, Congress is not bound by international law. If it chooses to do so, it may legislate with respect to conduct outside the United States in excess of the limits posed by international law"); *United States v. Felix-Gutierrez*, 940 F.2d 1200, 1203 (9th Cir. 1991); *United States v. Henriquez*, 731 F.2d 131, 134 (2d Cir. 1984). The one exception may apply in those instances where Congress's legislative authority cannot be claimed on the basis its constitutionally enumerated powers and must instead rest upon its authority to carry into effect the powers of sovereignty, cf. *United States v. Curtiss-Wright Export Corp.*, 299 U.S. 304, 318 (1936).

[47] "An analysis ... discloses five general principles on which a more or less extensive penal jurisdiction is claimed by States at the present time. These five general principles are: first, the *territorial principle*, determining jurisdiction by reference to the place where the offence

is committed; second, the *nationality principle*, determining jurisdiction by reference to the nationality or national character of the person committing the offence; third, the *protective principle*, determining jurisdiction by reference to the national interest injured by the offence; fourth, the *universality principle*, determining jurisdiction by reference to the custody of the person committing the offence; and fifth, the *passive personality principle*, determining jurisdiction by reference to the nationality or national character of the person injured by the offence. Of these five principles, the first is everywhere regarded as of primary importance and of fundamental character. The second is universally accepted, though there are striking differences in the extent to which it is used in different national systems. The third is claimed by most States, regarded with misgivings in a few, and generally ranked as the basis for an auxiliary competence. The fourth is widely though by no means universally accepted as the basis of an auxiliary competence, except for the offence of piracy, with respect to which it is the generally recognized principle of jurisdiction. The fifth, asserted in some form by a considerable number of States and contested by others, is admittedly auxiliary in character and is probably not essential for any State if the ends served are adequately provided for on other principles." Harvard Research in International Law, *Jurisdiction with Respect to Crime*, 29 AMERICAN JOURNAL OF INTERNATIONAL LAW (Supp.)(*Harvard Study*) 439, 445 (1935) (emphasis added).

48 "The rules in this Restatement governing jurisdiction to prescribe, as well as those governing jurisdiction to adjudicate and to enforce, reflect development in the law as given effect by United States courts. The courts appear to have considered these rules as a blend of international law and domestic law, including international 'comity' as part of that law. Increasingly, however, these rules, notably the principle of reasonableness (§§403, 421, 431), have been followed by other states and their courts and by international tribunals, and have emerged as principles of customary law." American Law Institute, 1 RESTATEMENT OF THE LAW THIRD: THE FOREIGN RELATIONS LAW OF THE UNITED STATES, 231 (1985). Section 403 of the Restatement provides:

"(2) Whether exercise of jurisdiction over a person or activity is unreasonable is determined by evaluating all relevant factors, including, where appropriate: (a) the link of the activity to the territory of the regulated state, i.e., the extent to which the activity takes place within the territory, or has substantial, direct, and foreseeable effect upon or in the territory; (b) the connections, such as nationality, residence, or economic activity, between the regulating state and the person principally responsible for the activity to be regulated, or between that state and those whom the regulation is designed to protect; (c) the character of the activity to be regulated, the importance of regulation to the regulating state, the extent to which other states regulate such activities, and the degree to which the desirability of such regulation is generally accepted; (d) the existence of justified expectations that might be protected or hurt by the regulation; (e) the importance of the regulation to the international political, legal, or economic system; (f) the extent to which the regulation is consistent with the traditions of the international system; (g) the extent to which another state may have an interest in regulating the activity; and (h) the likelihood of conflict with regulation by another state.

"(3) When it would not be unreasonable for each of two states to exercise jurisdiction over a person or activity, but the prescriptions by the two states are in conflict, each state has an obligation to evaluate its own as well as the other state's interest in exercising jurisdiction, in light of all the relevant factors, Subsection (2); a state should defer to the other state if that state's interest is clearly greater." *Id.* at 244-45. The remainder of section 403 and other portions of the RESTATEMENT appear as an attachment to this report.

49 E.g., *United States v. MacAllister*, 160 F.3d 1304, 1308 (11th Cir. 1998).

50 Gibney, *The Extraterritorial Application of U.S. Law: The Perversion of Democratic Governance, the Reversal of Institutional Roles, and the Imperative of Establishing Normative Principles*, 19 BOSTON COLLEGE INTERNATIONAL & COMPARATIVE LAW REVIEW 297 (1996); Abramovsky, *Extraterritorial Jurisdiction: The United States*

Unwarranted Attempt to Alter International Law in United States v Yunis, 15 YALE JOURNAL OF INTERNATIONAL LAW 121 (1990); *Exporting United States Drug Law: An Example of the International Legal Ramifications of the "War on Drugs,"* 1992 BRIGHAM YOUNG UNIVERSITY LAW REVIEW 165.

[51] *Harvard Study* at 480-509.

[52] E.g., 18 U.S.C. 81 (arson within the maritime and territorial jurisdiction of the United States), 113 (assaults within the maritime and territorial jurisdiction of the United States).

[53] *Ford v. United States*, 273 U.S. 593, 623 (1927)("a man who outside of a country willfully puts in motion a force to take effect in it is answerable at the place where the evil is done"); *United States v. Yousef*, 327 F.3d 56, 96-7 (2d Cir. 2003)("Moreover, assertion of jurisdiction is appropriate under the 'objective territorial principle' because the purpose of the attack was to influence United States foreign policy and the defendants intended their actions to have an effect –in this case, a devastating effect – on and within the United States"); *United States v. Neil*, 312 F.3d 419, 422 (9th Cir. 2002); *United States v. MacAllister*, 160 F.3d 1304, 1308 (11th Cir. 1998); *United States v. Goldberg*, 830 F.2d 459, 463-64 (3d Cir. 1987).

[54] *United States v. Felix-Gutierrez*, 940 F.2d 1200, 1205 (9th Cir. 1991)("Felix's actions created a significant detrimental effect in the United States and adversely affected the national interest. In helping to prevent the United States from apprehending Caro-Quintero, Felix directly hindered United States efforts to prosecute an alleged murderer of a government agent. Furthermore that agent was a United States citizen. We need not decide whether any one of these facts or principles, standing alone, would be sufficient. Rather, we hold that cumulatively applied they require the conclusion that giving extraterritorial effect to the accessory after the act statute in Felix's case does not violate international law principles"); *United States v. Suerte*, 291 F.3d 366, 370 (5th Cir. 2002); *United States v. Cardales*, 168 F.3d 548, 553 (1st Cir. 1999); *United States v. Benitez*, 741 F.2d 1312, 1316 (11th Cir. 1984).

[55] *Harvard Study* at 543.

[56] *United States v. Vilches-Navarrete*, 523 F.3d 1, 21-2 (1st Cir. 2008)("Under the protective principle of international law, Congress can punish crimes committed on the high seas regardless of whether a vessel is subject to the jurisdiction of the United States. Under the protective principle, a state has jurisdiction to prescribe a rule of law attaching legal consequences to conduct outside its territory that threatens its security as a state or the operation of its governmental functions, provided the conduct is generally recognized as a crime under the law of states that have reasonably developed legal systems"); see also, *United States v. al Kassar*, 660 F.3d 108, 118 (2d Cir. 2011).

[57] *United States v. Vasquez-Velasco*, 15 F.3d 833, 841 (9th Cir. 1994); *United States v. Felix-Gutierrez*, 940 F.2d 1200, 1206 (9th Cir. 1991); *United States v. Benitez*, 741 F.2d 1312, 1316 (11th Cir. 1984).

[58] *United States v. Yousef*, 327 F.3d 56, 97 (2d Cir. 2003) ("Finally, there is no doubt that jurisdiction is proper under the protective principle because the planned attacks were intended to affect the United States and to alter its foreign policy").

[59] *United States v. Romero-Galue*, 757 F.2d 1147, 1154 (11th Cir. 1985).

[60] *United States v. Marino-Garcia*, 679 F.2d 1373, 1381 fn. 14 (11th Cir. 1982) (citing cases in accord).

[61] *United States v. Banjoko*, 590 F.3d 1278, 1281 (11th Cir. 2009).

[62] *United States v. Campbell*, 798 F.Supp.2d 293, 296 (D.D.C. 2011).

[63] *Harvard Study* at 519; *United States v. Frank*, 599 F.3d 1221, 1233 (11th Cir. 2010); *United States v. Clark*, 435 F.3d 1100, 1106 (9th Cir. 2006); *United States v. Martinez*, 599 F.Supp.2d 784, 797 (W.D.Tex. 2009).

[64] *Blackmer v. United States*, 284 U.S. 421, 437 (1932)("With respect to such exercise of authority, there is no question of international law, but solely of the purport of municipal law which establishes the duties of the citizen in relation to his own government. While the legislation of the Congress, unless the contrary intent appears, is construed to apply only

within the territorial jurisdiction of the United States, the question of its application so far as citizens of the United States in foreign countries are concerned is one of construction, not of legislative power").

65 *United States v. Plummer*, 221 F.3d 1298, 1305-307(11th Cir. 2000)(nationality and territorial principles); *Chua Han Mow v. United States*, 730 F.2d 1308, 1312 (9th Cir. 1984)(territorial, protective and nationality principles); *United States v. Smith*, 680 F.2d 255, 257-58 (1st Cir. 1982)(territorial and nationality principles); *United States v. Martinez*, 599 F.Supp.2d 784, 800 (W.D.Tex. 2009)(nationality, passive personality, and territorial principles).

66 *Harvard Study* at 445.

67 *United States v. Yousef*, 327 F.3d 56, 96 (2d Cir. 2003)(passive personality and territorial principles)("consistent with the passive personality principle of customary international jurisdiction because each of these counts involved a plot to bomb United States-flag aircraft that would have been carrying United States citizens and crews and that were destined for cities in the United States"); *United States v. Hill*, 279 F.3d 731, 739 (9th Cir. 2002)("In the instance case, the territorial, national, and passive personality theories combine to sanction extraterritorial jurisdiction"); *United States v. Rezaq*, 134 F.3d 1121, 1133 (D.C.Cir. 1998)(protective and passive personality principles).

68 *United States v. Shi*, 525 F.3d 709, 722 (9th Cir. 2008); *Harvard Study* at 445.

69 *United States v. Caicedo*, 47 F.3d 370, 372 (9th Cir. 1995).

70 A list of the citations to such federal statutes is attached.

71 The text of 18 U.S.C. 7 which defines the term "special maritime and territorial jurisdiction of the United States" is attached.

72 1 Stat. 113 (1790)(outlawing manslaughter committed in a place "under the sole and exclusive jurisdiction of the United States" and murder committed "upon the high seas").

73 "In this chapter –

"(1) 'aircraft in flight' means an aircraft from the moment all external doors are closed following boarding—(A) through the moment when one external door is opened to allow passengers to leave the aircraft; or (B) until, if a forced landing, competent authorities take over responsibility for the aircraft and individuals and property on the aircraft.

"(2) 'special aircraft jurisdiction of the United States' includes any of the following aircraft in flight: (A) a civil aircraft of the United States. (B) an aircraft of the armed forces of the United States. (C) another aircraft in the United States. (D) another aircraft outside the United States—(i) that has its next scheduled destination or last place of departure in the United States, if the aircraft next lands in the United States; (ii) on which an individual commits an offense (as defined in the Convention for the Suppression of Unlawful Seizure of Aircraft) if the aircraft lands in the United States with the individual still on the aircraft; or (iii) against which an individual commits an offense (as defined in subsection (d) or (e) of article I, section I of the Convention for the Suppression of Unlawful Acts against the Safety of Civil Aviation) if the aircraft lands in the United States with the individual still on the aircraft. (E) any other aircraft leased without crew to a lessee whose principal place of business is in the United States or, if the lessee does not have a principal place of business, whose permanent residence is in the United States.

"(3) an individual commits an offense (as defined in the Convention for the Suppression of Unlawful Seizure of Aircraft) when the individual, when on an aircraft in flight—(A) by any form of intimidation, unlawfully seizes, exercises control of, or attempts to seize or exercise control of, the aircraft; or (B) is an accomplice of an individual referred to in subclause (A) of this clause," 49 U.S.C. 46501.

74 "The term 'customs waters' means, [1] in the case of a foreign vessel subject to a treaty or other arrangement between a foreign government and the United States enabling or permitting the authorities of the United States to board, examine, search, seize, or otherwise to enforce upon such vessel upon the high seas the laws of the United States, the waters within such distance of the coast of the United States as the said authorities are or may be so

enabled or permitted by such treaty or arrangement and, [2] in the case of every other vessel, the waters within four leagues of the coast of the United States," 19 U.S.C. 1709(c).

[75] 18 U.S.C. 7(6)("Any vehicle used or designed for flight or navigation in space and on the registry of the United States pursuant to the Treaty on Principles Governing the Activities of States in the Exploration and Use of Outer Space, Including the Moon and Other Celestial Bodies and the Convention on Registration of Objects Launched into Outer Space, while that vehicle is in flight, which is from the moment when all external doors are closed on Earth following embarkation until the moment when one such door is opened on Earth for disembarkation or in the case of a forced landing, until the competent authorities take over the responsibility for the vehicle and for persons and property aboard").

[76] "Whoever knowingly operates, or attempts or conspires to operate, by any means, or embarks in any submersible vessel or semi-submersible vessel that is without nationality and that is navigating or has navigated into, through, or from waters beyond the outer limit of the territorial sea of a single country or a lateral limit of that country's territorial sea with an adjacent country, with the intent to evade detection, shall be fined under this title, imprisoned not more than 15 years, or both," 18 U.S.C. 2285(a).

[77] "With respect to offenses committed by or against a national of the United States as that term is used in section 101 of the Immigration and Nationality Act – (A) the premises of United States diplomatic, consular, military or other United States Government missions or entities in foreign States, including the buildings, parts of buildings, and land appurtenant or ancillary thereto or used for purposes of those missions or entities, irrespective of ownership; and (B) residences in foreign States and the land appurtenant or ancillary thereto, irrespective of ownership, used for purposes of those missions or entities or used by United States personnel assigned to those missions or entities," 18 U.S.C. 7(9).

[78] "(a) Whoever engages in conduct outside the United States that would constitute an offense punishable by imprisonment for more than 1 year if the conduct had been engaged in within the special maritime and territorial jurisdiction of the United States – (1) while employed by or accompanying the Armed Forces outside the United States; or (2) while a member of the Armed Forces subject to chapter 47 of title 10 (the Uniform Code of Military Justice), shall be punished as provided for that offense.

"(b) No prosecution may be commenced against a person under this section if a foreign government, in accordance with jurisdiction recognized by the United States, has prosecuted or is prosecuting such person for the conduct constituting such offense, except upon the approval of the Attorney General or the Deputy Attorney General (or a person acting in either such capacity), which function of approval may not be delegated.

"(c) Nothing in this chapter may be construed to deprive a court-martial, military commission, provost court, or other military tribunal of concurrent jurisdiction with respect to offenders or offenses that by statute or by the law of war may be tried by a court-martial, military commission, provost court, or other military tribunal.

"(d) No prosecution may be commenced against a member of the Armed Forces subject to chapter 47 of title 10 (the Uniform Code of Military Justice) under this section unless – (1) such member ceases to be subject to such chapter; or (2) an indictment or information charges that the member committed the offense with one or more other defendants, at least one of whom is not subject to such chapter," 18 U.S.C. 3261.

[79] "(a) Whoever, while employed by or accompanying the Federal Government outside the United States, engages in conduct outside the United States that would constitute an offense under chapter 77 [relating to peonage, slavery and trafficking] or 117 [relating to transportation for illegal sexual activity] of this title if the conduct had been engaged in within the United States or within the special maritime and territorial jurisdiction of the United States shall be punished as provided for that offense.

"(b) No prosecution may be commenced against a person under this section if a foreign government, in accordance with jurisdiction recognized by the United States, has prosecuted or is prosecuting such person for the conduct constituting such offense, except upon the approval of the Attorney General or the Deputy Attorney General (or a person acting in either such capacity), which function of approval may not be delegated," 18 U.S.C. 3271.

[80] E.g., 18 U.S.C. 1203 (hostage taking); 18 U.S.C. 175 (biological weapons); 18 U.S.C. 1091 (genocide); 18 U.S.C. ch.113C (torture).

[81] E.g.,18 U.S.C. 1091(d)(2)("the alleged offender is a national of the United States ... ").

[82] E.g., 18 U.S.C. 2340A(b)(2)("There is jurisdiction over the activity prohibited in subsection(a) if ... (2) the alleged offender is present in the United States, irrespective of the nationality of the victim or alleged offender").

[83] E.g., 18 U.S.C. 1203 (It is not an offense under this section [relating to hostage taking] if the conduct required for the offense occurred outside the United States unless – (A) the offender or the person seized or detained is a national of the United States; (B) the offender is found in the United States; or (C) the governmental organization sought to be compelled is the Government of the United States").

[84] E.g., 18 U.S.C. 351(i)(relating to crimes of violence committed against Members of Congress, Supreme Court justices, and certain senior executive officials) ("There is extraterritorial jurisdiction over the conduct prohibited by this section").

[85] E.g., 18 U.S.C. 175c (variola virus)(committed by or against a U.S. national; committed in or affecting interstate or foreign commerce; committed against federal property).

[86] 46 U.S.C. 70501-70507.

[87] 46 U.S.C. 70503.

[88] "In this chapter, the term 'vessel subject to the jurisdiction of the United States' includes – (A) a vessel without nationality; (B) a vessel assimilated to a vessel without nationality, in accordance with paragraph (2) of article 6 of the 1958 Convention on the High Seas; (C) *a vessel registered in a foreign nation where the flag nation has consented or waived objection to the enforcement of United States law by the United States*; (D) a vessel located within the customs waters of the United States; (E) *a vessel located in the territorial waters of another nation, where the nation consents to the enforcement of United States law by the United States*; and (F) a vessel located in the contiguous zone of the United States, as defined in Presidential Proclamation 7219 of September 2, 1999, and (i) is entering the United States, (ii) has departed the United States, or (iii) is a hovering vessel as defined in section 491 of the Tariff Act of 1930 (19 U.S.C. 1401)," 46 U.S.C. 70502(c)(1); e.g., *United States v. Cardales-Luna*, 632 F.3d 731, 736-37 (1st Cir. 2011).

[89] "In this chapter, the term, "vessel without nationality" includes – (A) a vessel aboard which the master or person in charge makes a claim of registry, which claim is denied by the flag nation whose registry is claimed; (B) any vessel aboard which the master or person in charge fails, upon request of an officer of the United States empowered to enforce applicable provisions of United States law, to make a claim of nationality or registry for that vessel; and (C) a vessel aboard which the master or person in charge makes a claim of registry and the claimed nation of registry does not affirmatively and unequivocally assert that the vessel is of its nationality," 46 U.S.C. 70502(d)(1).

[90] E.g., *United States v. Olave-Valencia*, 371 F.Supp.2d 1224, 1226 (S.D. Cal. 2005)(Coast Guard interdiction 250 miles from the Honduras/Costa Rica border); *United States v. Valencia-Aguirre*, 409 F.Supp.2d 1358, 1360 (M.D.Fla. 2006)(Coast Guard interdiction from a Navy frigate off the Coast of Colombia); *United States v. Perlaza*, 439 F.3d 1149, 1152 (9th Cir. 2006) (Navy and Coast Guard ships engaged in drug interdiction in Pacific off the coasts of Ecuador, Colombia and Peru).

[91] *United States v. Ledesma-Cuesta*, 347 F.3d 527, 532 (3d Cir. 2003); *United States v. Moreno-Morillo*, 334 F.3d 819, 824 (9th Cir. 2003); cf., *United States v. Matos-Luchi*, 627 F.3d 1, 3 (1st Cir. 2010); contra, *United States v. Cardales-Luna*, 632 F.3d at 738-51(Torruella, J. dissenting).

[92] *United States v. Angulo-Hernández*, 565 F.3d 2, 10-11(1st Cir. 2009)("Due process does not require the government to prove a nexus between a defendant's criminal conduct and the

United States in a prosecution under MDLEA when the flag nation has consented to the application of United State law to the defendants"); *United States v. Suerte*, 291 F.3d 366, 375 (5th Cir. 2002); *United States v. Perez Oviedo*, 281 F.3d 400, 402-3 (3d Cir. 2002); *contra, United States v. Klimavicius-Viloria*, 144 F.3d 1249, 1257 (9th Cir. 1998).

93 *United States v. Perlaza*, 439 F.3d 1149, 1165-166 (9th Cir. 2006)("After hearing all the evidence as to its status at a pretrial hearing, the district court determined that the Go-Fast was a stateless vessel. We find that by not submitting this issue to the jury, the district court erred. The evidence relating to the Go-Fast's statelessness presents precisely the kind of disputed factual question that *Smith* [*United States v. Smith*, 282 F.3d 758 (9th Cir. 2002)] requires a jury to resolve"); *contra*, *United States v. Tinoco*, 304 F.3d 1088, 1110-111 and n.22 (11th Cir. 2002)("Hence, although factbound determinations may be involved, that does not automatically mean that the 46 U.S.C.App. 1903 jurisdictional issue has to be decided by the jury ... Consequently, even if questions under the 46 U.S.C.App. 1903 jurisdictional requirement may have a factual component, that component does not have to be resolved by the jury, given that, as we have explained, the jurisdictional requirement goes only to the court's subject matter jurisdiction and does not have to be treated as an element of a MDLEA substantive offense ... We also note that our rejection of the appellant's argument concerning the fact-bound nature of 46 U.S.C.App. 1903 jurisdictional determinations appears to put us in conflict with one of our sister circuits ... In *United States v. Smith* ... [t]he Ninth Circuit concluded that the district court erred by taking the issue of whether the §1903 jurisdictional requirement had been met completely away from the jury"); cf., *United States v. Matos-Luchi*, 627 F.3d at 5.

94 *United States v. Bowman*, 260 U.S. 94 (1922)(the nature and purpose of a statute indicate whether Congress intended it to apply outside of the United States).

95 *Ford v. United States*, 273 U.S. 593, 623 (1927)("a man who outside of a country willfully puts in motion a force to take effect in it is answerable at the place where the evil is done").

96 *United States v. MacAllister*, 160 F.3d 1304, 1308 n.8 (11th Cir. 1998)("On authority of *Bowman*, courts have routinely inferred congressional intent to provide for extraterritorial jurisdiction over foreign offenses that cause domestic harm").

97 *United States v. Layton*, 855 F.2d 1388, 1395-397 (9th Cir. 1988) (At the time of the murder of Congressman Ryan for which Layton was convicted the statute was silent as to its extraterritorial application; several years later Congress added an explicit extraterritorial provision, 18 U.S.C. 351(i)).

98 *United States v. Felix-Guiterrez*, 940 F.2d 1200, 1204-206 (9th Cir. 1991); *United States v. Benitez*, 741 F.2d 1312, 1316-317 (11th Cir. 1984). Attached is a list of citations to statutes that condemn acts of violence against officers and officials of the United States, that contain no express provisions concerning their geographical application but that apply overseas, if the same logic evidenced in the cases noted above is followed.

99 *United States v. Vasquez-Velasco*, 15 F.3d 833, 839 (9th Cir. 1994).

100 *United States v. Pizzarusso*, 388 F.2d 8, 9-10 (2d Cir. 1968); *Rocha v. United States*, 288 F.2d 545, 549 (9th Cir. 1961); *United States v. Khale*, 658 F.2d 90, 92 (2d Cir. 1981); *United States v. Castillo-Felix*, 539 F.2d 9, 12-3 (9th Cir. 1976).

101 *United States v. Walczak*, 783 F.2d 852, 854-55 (9th Cir. 1986).

102 *United States v. Cotten*, 471 F.2d. 744, 749 (9th Cir. 1973)(U.S. citizen); *United States v. Ayesh*, 762 F.Supp.2d 832, 838-41 (E.D.Va. 2011)(foreign national).

103 *United States v. Birch*, 470 F.2d 808, 810-11 (4th Cir. 1972); *United States v. Fernandez*, 496 F.2d 1294, 1296 (5th Cir. 1954); *United States v. Aguilar*, 756 F.2d 1418, 1425 (9th Cir. 1985); *United States v. Castillo-Felix*, 539 F.2d 9, 12-3 (9th Cir. 1976).

104 *United States v. Leija-Sanchez*, 602 F.3d 797, 801-802 (7th Cir. 2010).

105 Attached are lists of the citations to the theft of federal property statutes, the destruction of federal property statutes, the federal false statement statutes, and the federal counterfeiting statutes.

106 *United States v. MacAllister*, 160 F.3d 1304, 1307-308 (11th Cir. 1998); *Ford v. United States*, 273 U.S. 593, 620-24 (1927); United States v. Inco Bank & Trust Corp., 845 F.2d 919, 920 (11th Cir. 1988); United States v. Manuel, 371 F.Supp.2d 404, 409 (S.D.N.Y. 2005).

107 *United States v. Felix-Gutierrez*, 940 F.2d 1200, 1204-207 (9th Cir. 1991)(accessory after the fact violation committed overseas). A list of citations to the piggyback offense statutes is attached.

108 E.g., 18 U.S.C. 2339D(b)(6) (relating to receipt of military training from a foreign terrorist organization)("(b) Extraterritorial jurisdiction – there is extraterritorial federal jurisdiction over an offense under this section. There is jurisdiction over an offense under subsection (a) if ... (6) an offender aids or abets any person over whom jurisdiction exists under this paragraph in committing an offense under subsection (a) or conspires with any person over whom jurisdiction exist under this paragraph to commit an offense under subjection (a)").

109 *United States v. Davis*, 905 F.2d 245, 249 (9th Cir. 1990); *United States v. Villanueva*, 408 F.3d 193, 197-99 (5th Cir. 2005).

110 The comparable question under state law is the extent to which a state's criminal law applies to activities occurring in another state.

111 See e.g., U.S. Const. Art.II, §2, cl.2 ("[t]he President ... shall have power, by and with the advice and consent of the Senate, to make treaties, provided two thirds of the Senators present concur; and he shall nominate, and by and with the advice and consent of the Senate, shall appoint Ambassadors, [and] other public ministers and consuls.... ");
U.S. Const. Art.II, §3, cl.3 (" ... he shall receive Ambassadors and other public ministers.... ");
U.S. Const. Art.II, §2, cl.1 ("[he] shall be commander in chief of the Army and Navy of the United States.... ");
U.S. Const. Art.I, §8, cl.18 ("[t]he Congress shall have power ... to make all laws which shall be necessary and proper for carrying into execution [its] powers, and all other powers vested by this Constitution in the Government of the United States, or in any Department or Officer thereof");
U.S. Const. Art.I, §8, cl.10 ("[t]he Congress shall have power ... to define and punish piracies and felonies committed on the high seas, and offences against the law of nations");
U.S. Const. Art.I, §8, cl.3 ("[t]he Congress shall have power ... to regulate commerce with foreign nations.... ");
U.S. Const. Art.I, §8, cl.1 ("[t]he Congress shall have power to lay and collect ... duties, imposts and excises, to pay the debts and provide for the common defence and general welfare.... ");
U.S. Const. Art.I, §8, cls.11, 12, 13, 14 ("[t]he Congress shall have power ... to declare war ... ; to raise and support armies ... ; to provide and maintain a navy ... ; [and] to make rules for the government and regulation of the land and naval forces.... ").

112 *Skiriotes v. Florida*, 313 U.S. 69, 77 (1941)("If the United States may control the conduct of its citizens upon the high seas, we see no reason why the State of Florida may not likewise govern the conduct of its citizens upon the high seas with respect to matters in which the State has a legitimate interest and where there is no conflict with acts of Congress"); *State v. Flores*, 218 Ariz. 407, 413-16, 188 P.3d 706, 712-15 (Ariz.App. 2009); *State v. Jack*, 125 P.3d 311, 318-19 (Alaska 2005); Colangelo, *Constitutional Limits on Extraterritorial Jurisdiction: Terrorism and the Intersection of National and International Law*, 48 HARVARD INTERNATIONAL LAW JOURNAL 121, 128 (2007).

113 "This Constitution, and the Laws of the United States which shall be made in pursuance thereof; and all treaties made, or which shall be made, under the authority of the United States, shall be the supreme law of the land; and the judges in every state shall be bound thereby; any thing in the constitution or laws of any state to the contrary notwithstanding," U.S. Const. Art.VI, cl.2.

[114] George, *Extraterritorial Application of Penal Legislation*, 64 MICHIGAN LAW REVIEW 609, 617 (1966); RESTATEMENT (THIRD) OF FOREIGN RELATIONS LAW §402 comment k, n.5 (1987).

[115] The Model Penal Code section (attached) exemplifies the standards found in most state extraterritorial criminal jurisdiction provisions. Several states have no general extraterritorial statute, but instead have statutory venue provisions indicating where criminal offenses with extraterritorial components may be tried, e.g., Ala.Code §15-2-3 ("When the commission of an offense commenced in the State of Alabama is consummated without the boundaries of the state, the offender is liable to punishment therefor in Alabama; and venue in such case is in the county in which the offense was commenced, unless otherwise provided by law").

[116] *Ala.Code §§15-2-3, 15-2-4; *Alaska Stat. §12.05.010; Ariz.Rev.Stat.Ann. §13-108(A)(1); Ark.Code Ann. §5-1- 104(a)(1); Cal.Penal Code §27(a)(1); Colo.Rev. Stat. §18-1-201(1)(a); Del.Code tit.11 §204(a)(1); Fla.Stat.Ann. §910.005(1)(a); Ga.Code §17-2-1(b)(1); Hawaii Rev.Stat. §701-106(1)(a); Idaho Code §18-202(1); Ill.Comp.Stat.Ann. ch.720, §5/1-5(a)(1); Ind. Code Ann. §35-41-1-1(b)(1); Iowa Code Ann. §803.1(1)(a); Kan.Stat.Ann. §21-3104; Ky.Rev.Stat. §500.060(1)(a); La.Code Crim.Pro. art. 611; Me.Rev.Stat.Ann. tit.17-A §7(1)(A); Minn.Stat.Ann. §609.025(1); *Miss.Code §§99-11-15, 99-11-17; Mo.Ann. Stat. §541.191(1)(1); Mont.Code Ann. §46-2-101; *Nev.Rev. Stat. §§170. 015, 170.020; N.H. Rev.Stat.Ann. §625:4(I)(a); N.J.Stat.Ann. §2C:1-3(a)(1); N.Y.Crim. Pro.Law §20.20(1)(a); *N.C.Gen.Stat. §15A-134; *N.D.Cent.Code §29-03-01; Ohio Rev.Code §2901.11(A)(1); Okla. Stat.Ann. tit.21 §151(1); Ore.Rev.Stat. §131.215(1); Pa.Stat.Ann. tit. 18 §102(a)(1); *S.D.Codified Laws §23A-16-2; *Tenn.Code Ann. §39-11-103(b); Tex. Penal Code §1.04 (a)(1); Utah Code Ann. §76-1-201(1)(a); Vt.Stat.Ann. tit.13 §2; Wash.Rev. Code Ann. §9A.04.030; Wis.Stat.Ann. §939.03 (1)(a).

*Statutes which phrase the extraterritorial jurisdiction statement in terms of offenses commenced in one state and consummated in another state, rather than in terms of elements.

[117] Ariz.Rev.Stat.Ann. §13-108(A)(2)(attempt and conspiracy); Ark.Code Ann.§5-1-104(a)(2),(3)(attempt and conspiracy); Colo. Rev.Stat. §18-1-201(1)(b),(c)(attempt and conspiracy); Del.Code tit.11 §204(a)(2)(conspiracy); Fla.Stat.Ann. §910.005 (1)(b),(c) (attempt and conspiracy); Ga.Code §17-2-1(b)(2)(attempt); Hawaii Rev.Stat. §701-106(1)(b),(c)(attempt and conspiracy); Ill.Comp.Stat.Ann. ch.720 §5/1-5(a)(2),(3) (attempt and conspiracy); Ind.Code Ann. §35-41-1-1(b)(2),(3)(attempt and conspiracy); Iowa Code Ann. §803.1(1)(b),(c)(attempt and conspiracy); Kan.Stat.Ann. §21-3104(1)(b),(c) (attempt and conspiracy); Ky.Rev.Stat. §500.060(1)(b),(c) (attempt and conspiracy); Me.Rev.Stat. Ann. tit.17-A, §7(1)(B), (C) (attempt and conspiracy); Mo.Ann.Stat. §541.191(1)(2) (attempt and conspiracy); Mont.Code Ann. §46-2-101(b)(attempt); N.H.Rev.Stat.Ann. §625:4(I)(b), (c) (attempt and conspiracy); N.J.Stat.Ann. §2C:1-3(a)(2),(3) (attempt and conspiracy); Ohio Rev.Code §2901.11 (A)(3) (attempt and conspiracy); Ore.Rev.Stat. §131.215(2), (3) (attempt and conspiracy); Pa. Stat.Ann. tit.18 §102(a)(2), (3) (attempt and conspiracy); Tex.Penal Code §1.04(a)(2), (3) (attempt and conspiracy); Utah Code Ann. §76-1-201(1)(b), (c) (attempt and conspiracy); Wis.Stat.Ann. §939.03(1)(b)(conspiracy).

[118] Ariz.Rev.Stat.Ann. §13-108(A)(3)(attempt and conspiracy); Ark.Code Ann.§5-1-104 (a)(4)(attempt and conspiracy); Colo. Rev.Stat. §18-1-201(1)(d)(attempt and conspiracy); Del.Code tit.11 §204(a)(3)(attempt and conspiracy); Fla.Stat.Ann. §910.005 (1)(d)(attempt and conspiracy); Ga.Code §17-2-1(b)(3)(attempt); Hawaii Rev.Stat. §701-106(1)(d) (attempt and conspiracy); Ill.Comp.Stat.Ann. ch.720 §5/1-5(1)(d)(attempt and conspiracy); Ind.Code Ann. §35-41-1-1(b)(4)(attempt and conspiracy); Iowa Code Ann. §803.1(1)(e) (attempt and conspiracy); Ky.Rev.Stat. §500.060(1)(d)(attempt and conspiracy); Me.Rev.Stat.Ann. tit.17-A, §7(1)(D) (attempt and conspiracy); Mo.Ann.Stat. §541.191(1)(3)(attempt and conspiracy); Mont.Code Ann. §46-2-101(c)(attempt and conspiracy); N.H.Rev. Stat.Ann. §625:4(I) (c); N.J.Stat.Ann. §2C:1-3(a)(4) (attempt and conspiracy); Ohio Rev.Code §2901.11(A)(2) (attempt and conspiracy); Ore.Rev.Stat.

§131.215(4) (attempt and conspiracy); Pa. Stat.Ann. tit.18 §102(a)(4)(attempt and conspiracy); R.I.Gen.Laws §11-1-7 (conspiracy); Tex.Penal Code §1.04(a) (3); Utah Code Ann. §76-1-201(1)(d)(attempt and conspiracy).

119 Ariz.Rev.Stat.Ann. §13-108(B); Ark.Code Ann. §5-1-104(b); Colo.Rev.Stat. §18-1-201(2); Del.Code tit.11 §204(c); Fla.Stat.Ann. §910.005(2); Ga.Code §17-2-1(c); Hawaii Rev.Stat. §701-106(4); Ill.Comp.Stat.Ann. ch.720 §5/1-5(b); Ind.Code Ann. §35-41-1-1(c); Iowa Code Ann. §803.1(2); Kan.Stat.Ann. §21-3104(2); Ky.Rev.Stat. §500.060(3); La.Code Crim.Pro. art. 611; Me. Rev.Stat.Ann. tit.17-A §7(3); Miss.Code §99-11-21; Mo. Ann.Stat. §541.191(2); Mont.Code Ann. §46-2-101(2); N.H.Rev.Stat.Ann. §625:4 (III); N.J.Stat. Ann.§2C:1-3(d); N.Y.Crim. Pro.Law §20.20(2)(a); Ohio Rev.Code §2901.11 (B); Ore.Rev. Stat. §131.235; Pa.Stat. Ann. tit.18 §102(c); Tex.Penal Code §1.04(b); Utah Code Ann. §76-1-201(3).

120 Ala.Code §15-2-5; Cal.Penal Code §27(a)(2); Idaho Code §18-202(2); Miss.Code §99-11-23; N.D.Cent.Code. §29-03-01.1; Ohio Rev.Code §2901.11(A)(5); Okla.Stat.Ann. tit.21 §151(2); R.I.Gen.Laws §12-3-7; Wash.Rev.Code Ann. §9A.04.030(2); Wis.Stat.Ann. §939.03(1)(d).

121 Ariz.Rev.Stat.Ann. §13-108(A)(4); Ark.Code Ann. §5-1-104(a)(5); Colo. Rev.Stat. §18-1-201(3); Del.Code tit.11 §204(4); Fla.Stat.Ann. §910.005(3); Ga. Code §17-2-1(d); Hawaii Rev.Stat. §701-106(1)(e); Ill.Comp.Stat.Ann. ch.720 §5/1-5(c); Ind. Code Ann. §35-41-1-1(b)(5); Iowa Code Ann. §803.1(3); Kan.Stat.Ann. §21-3104 (3); Ky.Rev.Stat. §500.060(1)(e); Me.Rev.Stat.Ann. tit.17-A §7(1)(E); Mo.Ann.Stat. §541.191(1)(4); Mont.Code Ann. §46-2-101(3); N.H.Rev.Stat.Ann. §625:4(I) (e); N.J.Stat.Ann. §2C:1-3(a)(5); Ohio Rev. Code §2901.11(A)(4); Ore.Rev.Stat. §131.215(5); Pa.Stat.Ann. tit.18 §102(a)(5); Tex.Penal Code §1.04(c); Utah Code Ann. §76-1-201(4).

122 RESTATEMENT (THIRD) OF FOREIGN RELATIONS LAW §432 cmt. c and rptrs.' n.1 (1986) ("In a case that received wide attention, two French customs officials traveled to Switzerland on several occasions in 1980 to interrogate a former official of a Swiss bank, with a view to gaining information about French citizens believed to be hiding funds from the French tax and exchange control authorities. The person interrogated informed the Swiss federal prosecutor's office, which caused the Swiss police to arrest the French officials on their next visit. The officials were convicted of committing prohibited acts in favor of a foreign state, as well as of violation of the Swiss banking and economic intelligence laws. Even though the two French defendants were engaged in official business on behalf of the government of a friendly foreign state, they were given substantial sentences").

123 See generally, Abbell, OBTAINING EVIDENCE ABROAD IN CRIMINAL CASES, ch.4 (2010). Jurisdictions with whom the United States has a bilateral mutual legal assistance treaty in force include Antigua and Barbuda, Argentina, Australia, Austria, Bahamas, Barbados, Belize, Belgium, Brazil, Bulgaria, Canada, China, Cyprus, the Czech Republic, Dominica, Egypt, Estonia, Finland, France, Germany, Greece, Grenada, Hong Kong, Hungary, Ireland, Israel, Italy, India, Jamaica, Japan, Korea, Latvia, Liechtenstein, Lithuania, Luxembourg, Malaysia, Mexico, Morocco, the Netherlands, Nigeria, Panama, the Philippines, Poland, Romania, Russia, St. Kitts & Nevis, St. Lucia, St. Vincent & the Grenadines, South Africa, Spain, Sweden, Switzerland, Thailand, Trinidad and Tobago, Turkey, the United Kingdom, the Cayman Islands, Anguilla, the British Virgin Islands, Montserrat, the Turks and Caicos Islands, Ukraine, Uruguay, and Venezuela, United States Department of State, TREATIES IN FORCE. (Jan. 1, 2011).

124 28 C.F.R. §0.64-1; *Treaty on Mutual Legal Assistance in Criminal Matters, U.S.-Egypt*, Arts. 1(3), S.Treaty Doc. 106-19 ("Assistance shall be provided in connection with any conduct that is the subject of the investigation, prosecution, or proceeding under the laws of the Requesting State"); *Treaty on Mutual Legal Assistance in Criminal Matters, U.S.-Greece*, Arts. 1(3), S.Treaty Doc. 106-18; *Treaty on Mutual Legal Assistance in Criminal Matters, U.S.-Cyprus*, Arts. 1(3), S.Treaty Doc. 106-20; *Treaty on Mutual Legal Assistance in Criminal Matters, U.S.-Cyprus,* Arts. 1(3),S.Treaty Doc. 106-35; *Treaty on Mutual Legal*

Assistance in Criminal Matters, U.S.-S.Afr., Arts. 1(3), S.Treaty Doc. 106-36. Under a few agreements, treaty benefits may not be available during preliminary investigations or for want of dual criminality, e.g., *Treaty on Mutual Legal Assistance in Criminal Matters, U.S.-Fr.*, Art. 1, S.Treaty Doc. 106-7 (" ... mutual assistance in investigations and proceedings in respect of criminal offenses the punishment of which, at the time of the request for assistance, is a matter for the judicial authorities of the Requesting State"); *Treaty on Mutual Legal Assistance in Criminal Matters, U.S.-Liech.*, Arts. 1, S.Treaty Doc. 107-16 ("Assistance shall be provided without regard to whether the conduct that is the subject of the investigation, prosecution, or proceeding in the Requesting State would constitute an offense under the laws of the Requested State, except that the Requested State may refuse to comply in whole or in part with a request for assistance to the extent that the conduct would not constitute an offense under its laws and the execution of the request would require a court order for search and seizure or other coercive measures").

[125] Ellis & Pisani, *The United States Treaties on Mutual Assistance in Criminal Matters: A Comparative Analysis*, 19 INTERNATIONAL LAWYER 189, 196-98 (1985); Nadelmann, *Negotiations in Criminal Law Assistance Treaties*, 33 AMERICAN JOURNAL OF COMPARATIVE LAW 467, 470-74 (1985).

[126] E.g., *Treaty on Mutual Legal Assistance in Criminal Matters, U.S.-Liech.*, Art. 13, S. Treaty Doc. 106-16 ("If the Requesting State seeks the location or identity of persons or items in the Requested State, the Requested State shall use its best efforts to ascertain the location or identity"); *Treaty on Mutual Legal Assistance in Criminal Matters, U.S.- Greece*, Art. 13, S.Treaty Doc. 106-18; *Treaty on Mutual Legal Assistance in Criminal Matters, U.S.-Egypt*, Art. 12, S.Treaty Doc. 106-19; *Treaty on Mutual Legal Assistance in Criminal Matters, U.S.-Rom.*, Art. 13, S.Treaty Doc. 106- 20; *Treaty on Mutual Legal Assistance in Criminal Matters, U.S.-Cyprus*, Art. 13, S.Treaty Doc. 106-35; *Treaty on Mutual Legal Assistance in Criminal Matters, U.S.-S.Afr.*, Art. 14, S.Treaty Doc. 106-36.

[127] E.g., *Treaty on Mutual Legal Assistance in Criminal Matters, U.S.-Fr.*, Art. 15, S. Treaty Doc. 106-17 ("The Requested State shall serve procedural documents and judicial decisions sent to it for this purpose by the Requesting State.... "); *Treaty on Mutual Legal Assistance in Criminal Matters, U.S.-Liech.*, Art. 14, S.Treaty Doc. 106-16; *Treaty on Mutual Legal Assistance in Criminal Matters, U.S.-Greece*, Art. 14, S.Treaty Doc. 106-18; *Treaty on Mutual Legal Assistance in Criminal Matters, U.S.-Egypt*, Art. 13, S.Treaty Doc. 106-19; *Treaty on Mutual Legal Assistance in Criminal Matters, U.S.-Rom.*, Art. 14, S.Treaty Doc. 106-20; *Treaty on Mutual Legal Assistance in Criminal Matters, U.S.-Cyprus*, Art. 14, S.Treaty Doc. 106-35; *Treaty on Mutual Legal Assistance in Criminal Matters, U.S.-S.Afr.*, Art. 15, S.Treaty Doc. 106-36.

[128] E.g., *Treaty on Mutual Legal Assistance in Criminal Matters, U.S.-Greece*, Art. 15, S.Treaty Doc. 106-18 (2000); ("The Requested State shall execute a request that it search for, seize, and transfer any item to the Requesting State if the request justifies such action under the laws of the Requested State.... "); *Treaty on Mutual Legal Assistance in Criminal Matters, U.S.-Liech.*, Art. 15, S.Treaty Doc. 106-16; *Treaty on Mutual Legal Assistance in Criminal Matters, U.S.-Fr.*, Art. 10, S. Treaty Doc. 106-17; *Treaty on Mutual Legal Assistance in Criminal Matters, U.S.-Egypt*, Art. 14, S.Treaty Doc. 106-19; *Treaty on Mutual Legal Assistance in Criminal Matters, U.S.-Rom.*, Art. 15, S.Treaty Doc. 106- 20 (2000); *Treaty on Mutual Legal Assistance in Criminal Matters, U.S.-Cyprus*, Art. 15, S.Treaty Doc. 106-35; *Treaty on Mutual Legal Assistance in Criminal Matters, U.S.-S.Afr.*, Art. 16, S.Treaty Doc. 106-36.

[129] E.g., *Treaty on Mutual Legal Assistance in Criminal Matters, U.S.-Egypt*, Art. 8, S.Treaty Doc. 106-19;("A person in the Requested State from whom testimony or evidence is requested pursuant to this Treaty shall be compelled, if necessary, under the laws of the Requested State to appear and testify or produce items, including documents, records, and articles of evidence ... "); *Treaty on Mutual Legal Assistance in Criminal Matters, U.S.-Liech.*, Art. 8, S.Treaty Doc. 106-16; *Treaty on Mutual Legal Assistance in Criminal*

Matters, U.S.-Fr., Art. 9(2), S. Treaty Doc. 106-17; *Treaty on Mutual Legal Assistance in Criminal Matters, U.S.-Greece*, Art. 8, S.Treaty Doc. 106-18; *Treaty on Mutual Legal Assistance in Criminal Matters, U.S.-Rom.*, Art. 8, S.Treaty Doc. 106-20; *Treaty on Mutual Legal Assistance in Criminal Matters, U.S.-Cyprus*, Art. 8, S.Treaty Doc. 106-35; *Treaty on Mutual Legal Assistance in Criminal Matters, U.S.-S.Afr.*, Art. 9, S.Treaty Doc. 106-36.

[130] E.g., *Treaty on Mutual Legal Assistance in Criminal Matters, U.S.-Belize*, Art. 10, S.Treaty Doc. 106-19 ("1. When the Requesting State requests the appearance of a person in that State, the Requested State shall invite the person to appear before the appropriate authority in the Requesting State ... "); see also, *Treaty on Mutual Legal Assistance in Criminal Matters, U.S.-Liech.*, Art. 10, S.Treaty Doc. 107-16 (person may be served or detained except as stated in the request); *Treaty on Mutual Legal Assistance in Criminal Matters, U.S.-Venez.*, Art. X, S.Treaty Doc. 105-38.

[131] E.g., *Treaty on Mutual Legal Assistance in Criminal Matters, U.S.-Cyprus*, Art. 17(2), S.Treaty Doc. 106-35 (2000) ("The Parties shall assist each other to the extent permitted by their respective laws in proceedings relating to the forfeiture of the proceeds and instrumentalities of offense, restitution to the victims of crime, and the collection of fines imposed as sentences in criminal prosecutions. This may include action to temporarily immobilize the proceeds or instrumentalities pending further proceedings"); *Treaty on Mutual Legal Assistance in Criminal Matters, U.S.-Greece*, Art. 17, S.Treaty Doc. 106-18 ; *Treaty on Mutual Legal Assistance in Criminal Matters, U.S.-Liech.*, Art. 17, S.Treaty Doc. 106-16; *Treaty on Mutual Legal Assistance in Criminal Matters, U.S.-Fr.*, Art. 11, S. Treaty Doc. 106-17; *Treaty on Mutual Legal Assistance in Criminal Matters, U.S.-Egypt*, Art. 16, S.Treaty Doc. 106-19; *Treaty on Mutual Legal Assistance in Criminal Matters, U.S.-Rom.*, Art. 17, S.Treaty Doc. 106-20; *Treaty on Mutual Legal Assistance in Criminal Matters, U.S.-S.Afr.*, Art. 18, S.Treaty Doc. 106-36.

[132] 28 U.S.C. 1781, 1782; F.R.Civ.P. 28(b).

[133] See generally, Abbell, OBTAINING EVIDENCE ABROAD IN CRIMINAL CASES §3-3 (2010); United States Department of State, *Preparation of Letters Rogatory*, available on December 7, 2009 at http://www.travel.state.gov/law/info/judicial/ judicial_683.html. One commentator has observed that, "parties utilizing letters rogatory must simply cross their fingers and hope that the foreign nation will provide the evidence in a timely fashion and in an admissible form. Historically, the absence of a reliable evidence-gathering mechanism often stymied prosecutorial efforts, making it not unusual for the U.S. government to simply forgo transnational prosecutions," Richardson, *Due Process for the Global Crime Age: A Proposal*, 41 CORNELL INTERNATIONAL LAW JOURNAL 347 (2008); see also, United States v. el-Mezain, 664 F.3d 467, 517 (5th Cir. 2011), quoting *Societe Nationale Industrielle Aerospatiale v. U.S. District Court*, 482 U.S. 522, 531 (1987)("The letter rogatory process has been described as 'complicated, dilatory, and expensive'").

[134] See generally, Abbell, OBTAINING EVIDENCE ABROAD IN CRIMINAL CASES §3-1 (2010).

[135] Ass't Att'y Gen. Lanny A. Breuer, *The Global Case for Justice: Protecting Human Rights and Promoting the Rule of Law* at http://www.justice.gov/criminal/pr/speeches/2009/10/10-07-09/breuer-speech.pdf.

[136] Federal Bureau of Investigation, *Legal Attache Offices* at http://www.fbi.gov/contact-us/legat/ legal_offices.

[137] Drug Enforcement Administration, *DEA Office Locations* at http://www.justice.gov/dea/ agency/domestic.htm.

[138] U.S. Immigration and Customs Enforcement, at http://www.ice.gov/about/offices/homeland-security-investigatons/ oia/.

[139] U.S. Secret Service, *U.S. Secret Service Field Offices* at http://www.secretservice.gov/field_ offices.shtml.

[140] U.S. Securities and Exchange Commission, *International Enforcement Assistance* at http:// www.sec.gov/about/offices/oia/oia_crossborder.htm#mechanisms. See also, http://www. iosco.org/library/index.cfm?section=mou_siglist.

[141] P.L. 111-79, 123 Stat. 2086 (2009), 18 U.S.C. 3512.

[142] 18 U.S.C. 3512(a)(2). In the absence of a treaty nexus, the reach of the authority may be subject to constitutional limitations, see U.S. Const. Art. III, §2.

[143] *United States v. Verdugo-Urquidez*, 494 U.S. 259 (1990).

[144] *United States v. Conroy*, 589 F.2d 1258, 1264 (5th Cir. 1979); *Berlin Democratic Club v. Rumsfeld*, 410 F.Supp. 144, 157 (D.D.C. 1976).

[145] *Birdsell v. United States*, 346 F.2d 775, 782 (5th Cir. 1965).

[146] *United States v. Janis*, 428 U.S. 433, 455-56 n.31 (1976)(" ... It is well established, of course, that the exclusionary rule, as a deterrent sanction, is not applicable where a private party or foreign government commits the offending act"); *United States v. Callaway*, 446 F.2d 753, 755 (3d Cir. 1971); *United States v. Morrow*, 537 F.2d 120, 139 (5th Cir. 1976); *Stowe v. Devoy*, 588 F.2d 336, 341 (2d Cir. 1978); *United States v. Marzano*, 537 F.2d 257, 269-71 (7th Cir. 1976); *United States v. Rose*, 570 F.2d 1358, 1361-362 (9th Cir. 1978); *United States v. Hensel*, 699 F.2d 18, 25 (1st Cir. 1983); *United States v. Mount*, 757 F.2d 1315, 1317-318 (D.C.Cir. 1985); *United States v. Delaplane*, 778 F.2d 570, 573 (10th Cir. 1985); *United States v. Rosenthal*, 793 F.2d 1214, 1231 (11th Cir. 1986).

[147] *Stonehill v. United States*, 405 F.2d 738, 743 (9th Cir. 1969)("Neither the Fourth Amendment to the United States Constitution nor the exclusionary rule of evidence, designed to deter federal officers from violating the Fourth Amendment, is applicable to the acts of foreign officials").

[148] *United States v. Callaway*, 446 F.2d 753, 755 (3d Cir. 1971); *United States v. Morrow*, 537 F.2d 120, 139 (5th Cir. 1976); *Stowe v. Devoy*, 588 F.2d 336, 341 (2d Cir. 1978); *United States v. Rose*, 570 F.2d 1358, 1362 (9th Cir. 1978); *United States v. Hensel*, 699 F.2d 18, 25 (1st Cir. 1983); *United States v. Delaplane*, 778 F.2d 570, 573-74 (10th Cir. 1985); *United States v. Rosenthal*, 793 F.2d 1214, 1231-232 (11th Cir. 1986).

[149] *Stonehill v. United States*, 405 F.2d 738, 743 (9th Cir. 1969); *United States v. Callaway*, 446 F.2d 753, 755 (3d Cir. 1971); *United States v. Morrow*, 537 F.2d 120, 139 (5th Cir. 1976); *United States v. Rose*, 570 F.2d 1358, 1362 (9th Cir. 1978); *United States v. Hensel*, 699 F.2d 18, 25 (1st Cir. 1983); *United States v. Mount*, 757 F.2d 1315, 1317-318 (D.C.Cir. 1985); *United States v. Delaplane*, 778 F.2d 570, 573-74 (10th Cir. 1985); *United States v. Rosenthal*, 793 F.2d 1214, 1231-232 (11th Cir. 1986).

[150] "We think that the text of the Fourth Amendment, its history, and our cases discussing the application of the Constitution to aliens and extraterritorially require rejection of respondent's claim. At the time of the search, he was a citizen and resident of Mexico with no voluntary attachment to the United States and the place searched was located in Mexico. Under these circumstances, the Fourth Amendment has no application," 494 U.S. 274-75.

[151] 494 U.S. at 278 (Kennedy, J., concurring)("The absence of local judges or magistrates available to issue warrants, the differing and perhaps unascertainable conceptions of reasonableness and privacy that prevail abroad, and the need to cooperate with foreign officials all indicate that the Fourth Amendment's warrant requirement should not apply in Mexico as it does in this country"); *id.* at 279 (Stevens, J., concurring in the judgment)("I do agree, however, with the Government's submission that the search conducted by the United States agents with the approval and cooperation of the Mexican authorities was not 'unreasonable' as that term is used in the first Clause of the Amendment. I do not believe the Warrant Clause has any application to searches of noncitizens' homes in foreign jurisdictions because American magistrates have no power to authorize such searches").

[152] *United States v. Valencia-Trujillo*, 573 F.3d 1171, 1183 (11th Cir. 2009); *United States v. Bravo*, 489 F.3d 1, 8-9 (1st Cir. 2007); *United States v. Zakharov*, 468 F.3d 1171, 1179-180 (9th Cir. 2006); *United States v. Inigo*, 925 F.3d 641, 656 (3d Cir. 1991).

[153] *United States v. Emmanuel*, 565 F.3d 1324, 1330 (11th Cir. 2009); *United States v. Barona*, 56 F.3d 1087, 1090-93 (9th Cir. 1995); *United States v. Behety*, 32 F.3d 503, 510-11 (11th Cir. 1994)(the Fourth Amendment does not apply to the search and seizure of alien property abroad by foreign officials subject to conscience shocking and joint venture exceptions);

United States v. Castro, 175 F.Supp.2d 129, 132-33 (D.P.R. 2001); *United States v. Marzook*, 435 F.Supp.2d 708, 774 (N.D. Ill. 2006).

[154] *In re Terrorist Bombings of U.S. Embassies in East Africa*, 552 F.3d 157, 167-72 (2d Cir. 2008); *United States v. Barona*, 56 F.3d 1087, 1094 (9th Cir. 1995).

[155] *United States v. Juda* 46 F.3d 961, 968 (9th Cir. 1995); *United States v. Castro*, 175 F.3d 129, 133-34 (D.P.R. 2001).

[156] *United States v. Frank*, 599 F.3d 1221, 1228 (11th Cir. 2010); *United States v. Abu Ali*, 528 F.3d 210, 227-28 (4th Cir. 2008); *United States v. Yousef*, 327 F.3d 56, 145 (2d Cir. 2003); *United States v. Martindale*, 790 F.2d 1129, 1131-132 (4th Cir. 1986); *United States v. Heller*, 625 F.2d 594, 599 (5th Cir. 1980); *United States v. Mundt*, 508 F.2d 904, 906 (10th Cir. 1974); *United States v. Karake*, 443 F.Supp.2d 8, 49 (D.D.C. 2006).

[157] *United States v. Frank*, 599 F.3d at 1228-229; *United States v. Abu Ali*, 528 F.3d 210, 227-28 (4th Cir. 2008); *United States v. Yousef*, 327 F.3d 56, 145-46 (2d Cir. 2003); *United States v. Heller*, 625 F.2d 594, 599 (5th Cir. 1980); *United States v. Covington*, 783 F.2d 1052, 1056 (9th Cir. 1986); *United States v. Mundt*, 508 F.2d 904, 906-907 (10th Cir. 1974); *United States v. Karake*, 443 F.Supp.2d 8, 49 (D.D.C. 2006); *United States v. Hensel*, 509 F.Supp. 1364, 1375 (D. Me. 1981).

[158] *United States v. Frank*, 599 F.3d at 1228; United *States v. Abu Ali*, 528 F.3d 210, 227-28 (4th Cir. 2008); *United States v. Yousef*, 327 F.3d 56, 145-46 (2d Cir. 2003), citing, *United States v. Cotroni*, 527 F.2d 708, 712 n.10 (2d Cir. 1975); *United States v. Heller*, 625 F.2d 594, 599 (5th Cir. 1980).

[159] *In re Terrorist Bombings of U.S. Embassies in East Africa*, 552 F.3d 177, 201-2 (2d Cir. 2008); *United States v. Clarke*, 611 F.Supp.2d 12, 28-9 (D.D.C. 2009); *United States v. Yousef*, 327 F.3d 56, 145-46 (2d Cir. 2003).

[160] *Schneckloth v. Bustamonte*, 412 U.S. 218, 225-26 (1973)("the ultimate test remains that which has been the only clearly established test in Anglo-American courts for two hundred years: the test of voluntariness. Is the confession the product of an essentially free and unconstrained choice by its maker? If it is, if he has will to confess, it may be used against him. If it is not, if his will has been overborne and his capacity for self-determination critically impaired, the use of confession offends due process"); *United States v. Abu Ali*, 528 F.3d 210, 232 (4th Cir. 2008); *United States v. Lopez*, 437 F.3d 1059, 1063-64 (10th Cir. 2006); *United States v. Jacobs*, 431 F.3d 99, 108 (3d Cir. 2005); *United States v. Thompson*, 422 F.3d 1285, 1295-296 (11th Cir. 2005); *United States v. Garcia Abrego*, 141 F.3d 142, 170-71 (5th Cir. 1998); *United States v. Karake*, 443 F.Supp.2d 8, 85-6 (D.D.C. 2006); *United States v. Marzook*, 435 F.Supp.2d 708, 741 (N.D.Ill. 2006)("interrogation accompanied by physical violence is presumptively involuntary").

[161] 18 U.S.C. 3282.

[162] 18 U.S.C. 3281 (capital offenses); 18 U.S.C. 3299 (felony violations of 18 U.S.C. chs. 109A, 110, 117 and sections 1201 (if the victim is a child) and 1591); 18 U.S.C. 3286(b)(prosecution of any of the offenses listed in 18 U.S.C. 2332b(g)(5)(B) whose commission created a foreseeable risk of serious injury or resulted in such injury). Section 2332b(g)(5)(B) lists more than 40 federal criminal offenses including crimes such as violence in international airports (18 U.S.C. 37), assassination of the President (18 U.S.C. 1751), providing material support to terrorist organizations (18 U.S.C. 2339B).

[163] 18 U.S.C. 3286(a)(violation of an offense listed in 18 U.S.C. 2332b(g)(5)(B) whose commission does not create a foreseeable risk of serious injury or result in such injury).

[164] 18 U.S.C. 3290. Most courts construe section 3290 to require flight with an intent to avoid prosecution or a departure from the place where the offense occurred with the knowledge that an investigation is pending or being conducted, *United States v. Florez*, 447 F.3d 145, 150-52 (2d Cir. 2006)(citing authority in accord). Thus, a suspect in the case of an federal extraterritorial offense is not likely to be considered a fugitive, if he simply remains in the country were of the offense was committed.

[165] 18 U.S.C. 3292(c)("The total of all periods of suspension under this section with respect to an offense – (1) shall not exceed three years; and (2) shall not extend a period within which a criminal case must be initiated for more than six months if all foreign authorities take final action before such period would expire without regard to this section"); *United States v. Jenkins*, 633 F.3d 788, 797 (9th Cir. 2011); *United States v. Baldwin*, 414 F.3d 791, 795 (7th Cir. 2005); *United States v. Grenoble*, 413 F.3d 569, 574-75 (6th Cir. 2005).

[166] 18 U.S.C. 3292(b).

[167] *United States v. Lyttle*, ___ F.3d ___, ___ (2d Cir. Feb. 6, 2012); *United States v. Jenkins*, 633 F.3d 788, 797-98 (9th Cir. 2011); *United States v. Tainor*, 376 F.3d 1325, 1332-334 (11th Cir. 2004).

[168] *United States v. Hagege*, 437 F.3d 943, 955 (9th Cir. 2006).

[169] *United States v. Jenkins,* 633 F.3d 788, 799 (9th Cir. 2011)(emphasis added)("[T]he only temporal requirements of a §3292 application are (1) that the *official request* for evidence in a foreign country be made before the statute of limitations expires and (2) that the application for suspension be submitted to the district court before the indictment is filed"); *United States v. Kozeny*, 541 F.3d 166, 174 (2d Cir. 2008)(emphasis added)("We therefore conclude that the plain language of 18 U.S.C. §3292 requires that an *application* to suspend the running of the statute of limitations be filed before the limitations period has expired"); *United States v. Hoffecker*, 530 F.3d 137, 163 n.4 (3d Cir. 2008)("[T]here is no reason why a case seemingly barred by the statute of limitations cannot be revived by a §3292 application made before the Government has received all of the requested foreign evidence").

[170] *United States v. Atiyeh*, 402 F.3d 354, 362-66 (3d Cir. 2005)(holding that the statute of limitations may not be suspended under section 3292 when the request for foreign assistance is submitted after the evidence has in fact been received); *contra*, *United States v. Miller*, 830 F.2d 1073, 1076 (9th Cir. 1987); *United States v. DeGeorge*, 380 F.3d 1203, 1213 (9th Cir. 2004).

[171] *United States v. DeGeorge*, 380 F.3d 1203, 1214 (9th Cir. 2004).

[172] See generally, CRS Report 98-958, *Extradition To and From the United States: Overview of the Law and Recent Treaties*, by Michael John Garcia and Charles Doyle.

[173] 18 U.S.C. 3181 note (list the countries with whom we have extradition treaties).

[174] Abbell, EXTRADITION TO AND FROM THE UNITED STATES, §§3-2(5), 6-2(5) (2010).

[175] E.g., *Extradition Treaty, U.S.-Jordan*, Art.2(4), S.Treaty Doc. 104-3 ("An offense described in this Article shall be an extraditable offense regardless of where the act or acts constituting the offense were committed"); *Extradition Treaty, U.S.-Austria*, Art.2(6), S.Treaty Doc. 105-50; *Extradition Treaty, U.S.-Lux.*, Art.2(1), S.Treaty Doc. 105-10.

[176] *Extradition Treaty, U.S.-Hung.*, Art.2(4), S.Treaty Doc. 104-5 ("If the offense has been committed outside the territory of the Requesting State, extradition shall be granted if the laws of the Requested State provide for the punishment of an offense committed outside of its territory in similar circumstances. If the laws of the Requested State do not so provide, the executive authority of the Requested State may, in its discretion grant extradition"); *Extradition Treaty, U.S.-Bah.*, Art.2(4), S.Treaty Doc. 102-17.

[177] *Extradition Treaty, U.S.-Fr.,* Art.2(4), S.Treaty Doc. 105-13 ("Extradition shall be granted for an extraditable offense committed outside the territory of the Requesting State, when the laws of the Requested State authorize the prosecution or provide the punishment for that offense in similar circumstances").

[178] Bassiouni, INTERNATIONAL EXTRADITION: UNITED STATES LAW AND PRACTICE 739 (5th ed. 2007).

[179] E.g., *Extradition Treaty, U.S.-Peru*, Art. III, S.Treaty Doc. 107-6 ("Extradition shall not be refused on the ground that the person sought is a national of the Requested State"); *Extradition Treaty, U.S.-Belize*, Art. 3, S.Treaty Doc. 106-38; *Extradition Treaty, U.S.-Para.*, Art. III, S.Treaty Doc. 106-4.

[180] *Extradition Treaty, U.S.-Kor.*, Art. 3, S.Treaty Doc. 106-2 ("1. Neither Contracting State shall be bound to extradite its own nationals, but the Requested State shall have the power to extradite such person if, in its discretion, it be deemed proper to do so. 2. If extradition is refused solely on the basis of the nationality of the person sought, the Requested State shall, at the request of the Requesting State, submit the case to its authorities for prosecution. 3. Nationality shall be determined at the time of the commission of the offense for which extradition is requested"); *Extradition Treaty, U.S.-Pol.*, Art. 4, S.Treaty Doc. 105-14; *Extradition Treaty, U.S.-Fr.*, Art. 3, S.Treaty Doc. 105-13.

[181] Bassiouni, INTERNATIONAL EXTRADITION: UNITED STATES LAW AND PRACTICE 651 (5th ed. 2007).

[182] *Quinn v. Robinson*, 783 F.2d 776, 792-93 (9th Cir. 1986)("The political offense exception is premised on a number of justifications. First, its historical development suggests that it is grounded on the belief that individuals have a right to resort to political activism to foster political change. This justification is consistent with the modern consensus that political crimes have greater legitimacy than common crimes. Second, the exception reflects a concern that individuals– particularly unsuccessful rebels – should not be returned to countries where they may be subjected to unfair trials and punishments because of their political opinions. Third, the exception comports with the notion that governments – and certainly their non-political branches – should not intervene in the internal political struggles of other nations").

[183] Bassiouni, INTERNATIONAL EXTRADITION: UNITED STATES LAW AND PRACTICE 650-732 (5th ed. 2007).

[184] E.g., *Extradition Treaty, U.S.-S.Afr.*, Art. 4, S.Treaty Doc. 106-24 ("1. Extradition shall not be granted if the offense for which extradition is requested is a political offence. 2. For the purpose of this Treaty, the following offenses shall not be considered political offenses: (a) a murder or other violent crime against a Head of State or Deputy Head of State of the Requesting or Requested State, or against a member of such person's family; (b) an offence for which both the Requesting and Requested States have the obligation pursuant to a multilateral international agreement to extradite the person sought or to submit the case to their respective competent authorities for decision as to prosecution; (c) murder; (d) an offense involving kidnaping, abduction, or any form of unlawful detention, including the taking of a hostage; and (e) attempting or conspiring to commit, aiding, abetting, inducing, counseling or procuring the commission of, or being an accessory before or after the fact of such offences. 3. Notwithstanding the terms of subarticle 2, extradition shall not be granted if the executive authority of the Requested State determines that there are substantial grounds for believing that the request has been made for the purpose of prosecuting or punishing a person on account of that person's gender, race, religion, nationality, or political opinion"); *Extradition Treaty, U.S.-Pol.*, Art. 5, S.Treaty Doc. 105-14 (motivation clause is limited to politically motivated); *Extradition Treaty, U.S.-Sri Lanka*, Art. 4, S.Treaty Doc. 106-34 (only Heads of State clause, clauses identifying particular international obligations, and a conspiracy-attempt-accessory clause)(motivation clause is limited to politically motivated requests).

[185] Abbell, EXTRADITION TO AND FROM THE UNITED STATES, §3-2(2)(2010).

[186] 8 Stat. 116, 129 (1794).

[187] *Extradition Treaty, U.S.-U.K.*, 28 U.S.T. 227, 235(1977)(29 crimes); *Extradition Treaty, U.S.-Nor.*, 31 U.S.T. 5619, 5634 (1980)(33 crimes); *Extradition Treaty, U.S.-F.R.G.*, 32 U.S.T. 1485, 1515 (1980)(33 crimes).

[188] E.g., *Extradition Treaty, U.S.-Austria*, Art. 2(1), S.Treaty Doc. 105-50 ("Extradition shall be granted for offenses which are subject under the laws in both Contracting Parties by deprivation of liberty for a period of more than one year or by a more severe penalty"); *Extradition Treaty, U.S.-Malay.*, Art. 2(1), S.Treaty Doc. 104-26; *Extradition Treaty, U.S.-Zimb.*, Art. 2(1), S.Treaty Doc. 105-33.

[189] *United States v. Mejia*, 448 F.3d 436, 439 (D.C.Cir. 2006)(Panamaian authorities arrested the defendants and turned them over to U.S. Drug Enforcement Administration (DEA) officers in Panama who flew them to the U.S.); *United States v. Arbane*, 446 F.3d 1223, 1225 (11th Cir. 2006)(Ecuadorian officials deported the defendant to Iran on a plane scheduled to stop in the U.S. where the defendant was arrested); *United States v. Matta-Ballesteros*, 71 F.3d 754, 761 (9th Cir. 1995)(Honduran military and U.S. Marshals seized the defendant in Honduras and the Marshals flew him to the U.S. by way of the Dominican Republic); *United States v. Chapa-Garza*, 62 F.3d 118, 120 (5th Cir. 1995)(Mexican authorities deported the defendant to the United States); *United States v. Pomeroy*, 822 F.2d 718, 720 (8th Cir. 1987) (Canadian authorities deported the defendant to the United States); *United States v. Valot*, 625 F.2d 308, 309 (9th Cir. 1980)(Thai immigration authorities handed the defendant over to DEA agents in the Bangkok airport who flew him to the United States "over his protest").

[190] *United States v. Alvarez-Machain*, 504 U.S. 655, 669-70 (1992)(portions of the footnote 23 of the Court's opinion in brackets)("Mexico has protested the abduction of respondent through diplomatic notes, and the decision of whether respondent should be returned to Mexico, as a matter outside of the Treaty, is a matter for the Executive Branch. [The Mexican Government has also requested from the United States the extradition of two individuals it suspects of having abducted respondent in Mexico on charges of kidnaping. ...] ... The fact of respondent's forcible abduction does not therefore prohibit his trial in a court in the United States for violations of the criminal laws of the United States"); see also, *United States v. Struckman*, 611 F.3d 560, 571 (9th Cir. 2010)(internal citations omitted)("[T]he manner by which a defendant is brought to trial does not affect the government's ability to try him. We have, however, recognized exceptions to the *Ker/Frisbie* doctrine if either: (1) the transfer of the defendant violated the applicable extradition treaty, or (2) the United States government engaged in misconduct of the most shocking and outrageous kind to obtain his presence"); *United States v. Mejia*, 448 F.3d 436, 442-43 (D.C.Cir. 2006); *United States v. Arbane*, 446 F.3d 1223, 1225 (11th Cir. 2006); *United States v. Best*, 304 F.3d 308, 311-16 (3d Cir. 2002); *Kasi v. Angelone*, 300 F.3d 487, 493- 98 (4th Cir. 2002); *United States v. Torres Gonzalez*, 240 F.3d 14, 16 (1st Cir. 2001).

[191] U.S. Const. Art. III, §2, cl.3; Amend.VI.

[192] "The trial of all offenses begun or committed upon the high seas, or elsewhere out of the jurisdiction of any particular State or district, shall be in the district in which the offender, or any one of two or more joint offenders, is arrested or is first brought; but if such offender or offenders are not so arrested or brought into any district, an indictment or information may be filed in the district of the last known residence of the offender or of any one of two or more joint offenders, or if no such residence is known the indictment or information may be filed in the District of Columbia," 18 U.S.C. 3238. *United States v. Hisin-Yung*, 97 F.Supp.2d 24, 28 (D.C.Cir. 2000)("The two clauses provide alternative proper venues. Therefore, if the latter provision is relied on, and defendant is indicted before he is brought into the United States, he may be tried in the district in which he was indicted regardless of whether it is the district in which he is first brought into the United States"); see also, *United States v. Gurr*, 471 F.3d 144, 155 (D.C. Cir. 2007); *United States v. Hilger*, 867 F.2d 566, 568 (9th Cir. 1989); *United States v. Fraser*, 709 F.2d 1556, 1558 (6th Cir. 1983); *United States v. McRary*, 616 F.2d 181, 185 (5th Cir. 1980).

[193] *United States v. Feng*, 277 F.3d 1151, 1155 (9th Cir. 2002)("The word 'brought' under the statute means first brought into a jurisdiction from outside the United States jurisdiction while in custody"); *United States v. Catino*, 735 F.2d 718, 724 (2d Cir. 1984).

[194] 18 U.S.C. 3238 (" ... or any one of two or more joint offenders ... "). *United States v. Stickle*, 454 F.3d 1265, 1272- 273 (11th Cir. 2006); *United States v. Yousef*, 327 F.3d. 56, 115 (2d Cir. 2003).

[195] *United States v. Pendleton*, 658 F.3d 299, 304-305 (3d Cir. 2011)("[T]wo of our sister courts of appeals have held that '[s]ection 3238 does not apply unless the offense was committed

entirely on the high seas or outside the United States.' *United States v. Pace*, 314 F.3d 344, 351 (9th Cir. 2002); *United States v. Gilboe*, 684 F.2d 235 (2d Cir. 1982).... On the other hand, the Courts of Appeals for the Fourth and Fifth Circuits have held that §3238 applies even when some of a defendant's offense conduct takes place in the United States. See e.g. *United States v. Levy Auto Parts*, 787 F.2d 946, 950-52 (4th Cir. 1986)(finding venue proper under §3238 when conspiracy was 'essentially foreign,' even when some overt acts occurred inside the United States); *United States v. Erwin*, 602 F.2d 1183, 1185 (5th Cir. 1979)('That venue may also be appropriate in another district will not divest venue properly established under §3238.').... Although the title of §3238 includes only 'offenses not committed in any district,' it is a 'well-settled rule of statutory interpretation that titles and section headings cannot limit the plain meaning of statutory text where that text is clear.' ... Here, the plain language of §3238 supports the Fourth and Fifth Circuits' interpretation of the statute.... Here, although Pendleton's offense began when he initiated foreign travel by boarding a plane bound for Germany in the Eastern District of New York, he 'committed' the offense when he engaged in an illicit sex act in Germany. Because Pendleton's criminal conduct was 'essentially foreign,' *Levy Auto Parts*, 787 at 950, the District Court did not err in applying §3238 to hold that venue was proper in the district of arrest").

196 28 U.S.C. 1783 ("A court of the United States may order the issuance of a subpoena requiring the appearance as a witness before it, or before a person or body designated by it, of a national or resident of the United States who is in a foreign country, or requiring the production of a specified document or other thing by him, if the court finds that particular testimony or the production of the document or other thing by him is necessary in the interest of justice, and, in other than a criminal action or proceeding, if the court finds, in addition, that it is not possible to obtain his testimony in admissible form without his personal appearance or to obtain the production of the document or other thing in any other manner"); *Blackmer v. United States*, 284 U.S. 421, 436-38 (1932).

197 *United States v. Abu Ali*, 528 F.3d 210, 239 (4th Cir. 2008); *United States v. Yates*, 345 F.3d 1280, 1283 (11th Cir. 2003); *United States v. Olafson*, 213 F.3d 435, 441 (9th Cir. 2000); *United States v. Groos*, 616 F.Supp.2d 777, 791 (N.D.Ill. 2008); *United States v. Ozsusamlar*, 428 F.Supp.2d 161, 177 (S.D.N.Y. 2006); *cf.*, *United States v. Liner*, 435 F.3d 920, 924 (8th Cir. 2006). Cases where the witness is in federal custody overseas may prove an exception to the rule, but they may also come with their own special complications, see e.g., *United States v. Moussaoui*, 382 F.3d 453 (4th Cir. 2004)(foreign nationals held in military custody overseas whom the government, in the interest of national security, declined to make available for depositions or to appear as witnesses in a criminal trial).

198 E.g., *Treaty on Mutual Legal Assistance in Criminal Matters, U.S.-Leich.*, Art. 11, S.Treaty Doc. 107-16 ("1. A person in the custody of the Requested State whose presence outside of the Requested State is sought for purposes of assistance under this Treaty shall be transferred form the Requested State for that purpose if the person consents and if the Central Authorities of both States agree ... 3. For purposes of this Article: a) the receiving State shall have the authority and the obligation to keep the person transferred in custody unless otherwise authorized by the sending State; b) the receiving State shall return the person transferred to the custody of the sending State as soon as circumstances permit or as otherwise agreed by both Central Authorities; c) the receiving state shall not require the sending State to initiate extradition proceedings for the return of the person transferred; d) the person transferred shall receive credit for service of the sentence imposed in the sending State for time served in the custody of the receiving State; and e) where the receiving State is a third State the Requesting State shall be responsible for all arrangements necessary to meet the requirements of this paragraph"); see also, *Treaty on Mutual Legal Assistance in Criminal Matters, U.S.-Ukr.*, Art. 11, S.Treaty Doc. 106-16; *Treaty on Mutual Legal Assistance in Criminal Matters, U.S.-Fr.*, Art. 18, S.Treaty Doc. 106- 17; *Treaty on Mutual Legal Assistance in Criminal Matters, U.S.-Greece*, Art. 11, S.Treaty Doc. 106-18.

[199] E.g., *Treaty on Mutual Legal Assistance in Criminal Matters, U.S.-Belize*, Art. 10, S.Treaty Doc. 106-19 ("1. When the Requesting State requests the appearance of a person in that State, the Requested State shall invite the person to appear before the appropriate authority in the Requesting State. The Requesting State shall indicate the extent to which the expenses will be paid. The Central Authority of the Requested State shall promptly inform the Central Authority of the Requesting State of the response of the person. 2. The Central Authority of the Requesting state shall inform the Central Authority of the requested State whether a decision has been made by the competent authorities of the Requesting State that a person appearing in the Requesting State pursuant to this article shall not be subject to service of process, or be detained or subject to any restriction of personal liberty, by reason of any acts or convictions which preceded his departure from the Requested State"); see also, *Treaty on Mutual Legal Assistance in Criminal Matters, U.S.-Liech.*, Art. 10, S.Treaty Doc. 107-16 (person may not be served or detained except as stated in the request); *Treaty on Mutual Legal Assistance in Criminal Matters, U.S.-Venez.*, Arts. X, S.Treaty Doc. 105-38. When a witness is found in a country with whom the United States has no such treaty, officials have used U.S. immigration parole authority in an effort to accomplish the same results, see e.g., *Wang v. Reno*, 81 F.3d 808, 811-12 (9th Cir. 1996).

[200] F.R.Crim.P. 15(a)(1)("A party may move that a prospective witness be deposed in order to preserve testimony for trial. The court may grant the motion because of exceptional circumstances and in the interest of justice. If the court orders the deposition to be taken, it may also require the deponent to produce at the deposition any designated material that is not privileged, including any book, paper, document, record, recording, or data").

[201] F.R.Crim.P. 15(a), 18 U.S.C.App. (1964 ed.). For a history of the evolution of Rule 15 see, 2 WRIGHT, FEDERAL PRACTICE AND PROCEDURE §251 (Crim. 3d 2000).

[202] F.R.Crim.P. 15(a), 18 U.S.C.App. (1976 ed.); see also 18 U.S.C. 3503 (1970 ed.).

[203] "A witness who is detained under 18 U.S.C. § 3144 may request to be deposed by filing a written motion and giving notice to the parties. The court may then order that the deposition be taken and may discharge the witness after the witness has signed under oath the deposition transcript," F.R.Crim.P. 15(a)(2).

[204] *United States v. Liner*, 435 F.3d 920, 924 (8th Cir. 2006); see also, *United States v. Kelley*, 36 F.3d 1118, 1125 (D.C. Cir. 1994)(identifying the two as "critical factors"); *United States v. Jefferson*, 594 F.Supp.2d 655, 664 (E.D.Va. 2009).

[205] *United States v. Cohen*, 260 F.3d 68, 78 (2d Cir. 2001); see also, *United States v. Ruiz-Castro*, 92 F.3d 1519, 1533 (10th Cir. 1996)(identifying the three factors as among those a court should consider before authorizing depositions); *United States v. Thomas*, 62 F.3d 1332, 1341 (11th Cir. 1995)(listing consideration of unavailability, materiality, and "countervailing factors [that] would make the deposition unjust to the nonmoving party"); *United States v. Aggarwal*, 17 F.3d 737, 742 (5th Cir. 1994)(denial of the motion may be based entirely upon the fact it is untimely); *United States v. Jefferson*, 594 F.Supp.2d at 664-65 (failure of justice and all the circumstances); *United States v. Warren*, 713 F.Supp.2d 1, 3-4(D.D.C. 2010)("The defendant must also make some showing beyond unsubstantiated speculation, that the evidence exculpates him").

[206] *United States v. McKeeve*, 131 F.3d 1, 8 (1st Cir. 1997).

[207] "(e) Unless these rules or a court order provides otherwise, a deposition must be taken and filed in the same manner as a deposition in a civil action, except that (1) A defendant may not be deposed without that defendant's consent. (2) The scope and manner of the deposition examination and cross-examination must be the same as would be allowed during trial. (3) The government must provide to the defendant or the defendant's attorney, for use at the deposition, any statement of the deponent in the government's possession to which the defendant would be entitled at trial.

"(f) A party may use all or part of a deposition as provided by the Federal Rules of Evidence.

"(g) A party objecting to deposition testimony or evidence must state the grounds for the objection during the deposition, F.R.Crim.P. 15(e),(f),(g)(captions omitted).

208 "(1) The officer who has custody of the defendant must produce the defendant at the deposition and keep the defendant in the witness's presence during the examination, unless the defendant: (A) waives in writing the right to be present; or (B) persists in disruptive conduct justifying exclusion after being warned by the court that disruptive conduct will result in the defendant's exclusion. (2) A defendant who is not in custody has the right upon request to be present at the deposition, subject to any conditions imposed by the court. If the government tenders the defendant's expenses as provided in Rule 15(d) but the defendant still fails to appear, the defendant – absent good cause – waives both the right to appear and any objection to the taking and use of the deposition based on that right," F.R.Crim.P. 15(c)(captions omitted).

"If the deposition was requested by the government, the court may – or if the defendant is unable to bear the deposition expenses, the court must – order the government to pay: (1) any reasonable travel and subsistence expenses of the defendant and the defendant's attorney to attend the deposition; and (2) the costs of the deposition transcript,"F.R.Crim.P. 15(d)(captions omitted).

209 *Barber v. Page*, 390 U.S. 719, 725 (1968)("The right to confrontation is basically a trial right. It includes both the opportunity to cross-examine and the occasion for the jury to weigh the demeanor of the witness").

210 *United States v. McKeeve*, 131 F.3d 1, 8 (1st Cir. 1997); *United States v. Medjuck*, 156 F.3d 916, 920 (9th Cir. 1998); *United States v. Abu Ali*, 528 F.3d 210, 240 (4th Cir. 2008).

211 *United States v. McKeeve*, 131 F.3d 1, 8 (1st Cir. 1997)("the confrontation clause requires, at a minimum, that the government undertake diligent efforts to facilitate the defendant's presence. We caution, however, that although such efforts must be undertaken in good faith, they need not be heroic); *United States v. Kelly*, 892 F.2d 255, 262 (3d Cir. 1989); *United States v. Salim*, 855 F.2d 944, 950 (2d Cir. 1988).

212 *United States v. Johnpoll*, 739 F.2d 702, 710 (2d Cir. 1984)("The confrontation clause does not preclude admission of prior testimony of an unavailable witness, provided his unavailability is shown and the defendant had an opportunity to cross-examine. In the present case, Johnpoll had the full opportunity, at government expense, with his attorney to confront and cross-examine the Swiss witness, which he waived when he and his attorney decided not to attend the taking of the depositions").

213 *United States v. Sines*, 761 F.2d 1434, 1441 (9th Cir. 1985)("The Supreme Court has identified the major purposes of the confrontation clause as: (1) ensuring that witnesses will testify under oath; (2) forcing witnesses to undergo crossexamination; and (3) permitting the jury to observe the demeanor of witnesses. All three of these purposes were fulfilled when Steneman's videotaped deposition was taken [in Thailand] with Sine's attorney present").

214 *United States v. Medjuck*, 156 F.3d 916, 920 (9th Cir. 1998)("When the government is unable to secure a witness's presence at trial, Rule 15 is not violated by admission of videotaped testimony so long as the government makes diligent efforts to secure the defendant's physical presence at the deposition, and failing this, employs procedures that are adequate to allow the defendant to take an active role in the deposition proceedings ... The government was unable to secure Medjuck's presence at the Canadian depositions because there was no mechanism in place to allow United States officials to transfer Medjuck to Canadian authorities ... and secure his return to the United States in a timely fashion after the depositions. Finally, the government set up an elaborate system to allow Medjuck to witness the depositions live by video feed and to participate with his attorneys by private telephone connection during the depositions taken in Canada.... [A]n exception to the confrontation requirements] has been recognized for admission of deposition testimony where a witness is unavailable to testify at trial ... First, the deposition testimony must fall within an established exception to the hearsay rule. Second the deposition must be taken in compliance with law. Finally, the defendant must have had an opportunity to cross-examine

the deposed witness "); *United States v. Kelly*, 892 F.2d 255, 260-62 (3d Cir. 1980); *United States v. Walker*, 1 F.3d 423, 429 (6th Cir. 1993); *United States v. Mueller*, 74 F.3d 1152, 1156-157 (11th Cir. 1996); see also, *United States v. Salim*, 855 F.2d 944, 950 (2d Cir. 1988)("In the context of the taking of a foreign deposition, we believe that so long as the prosecution makes diligent efforts ... to attempt to secure the defendant's presence, preferably in person, but if necessary via some form of live broadcast, the refusal of the host government to permit the defendant to be present should not preclude the district court from ordering that the witness' testimony be preserved anyway. However, the district court should satisfy itself that defense counsel will be given an opportunity to cross-examine the witness in order to fulfill the mandate of Rule 15(b) to ensure a likelihood that the deposition will not violate the confrontation clause") .

215 *United States v. Sturman*, 951 F.2d 1466, 1480-481(6th Cir. 1992)("Swiss law forbids verbatim transcription so the summary method of establishing the record was the most effective legal method. All defense questions, with just one exception, were submitted to the witnesses so that objections and determinations on admissibility could be litigated later. Although the witnesses were not given an oath, defense conceded that each witness was told the penalties for giving false testimony ... Depositions taken in foreign countries cannot at all times completely emulate the United States methods of obtaining testimony. Here all steps were taken to ensure the defendants' rights while respecting the legal rules established in a different country").

216 E.g., *Treaty on Mutual Legal Assistance on Criminal Matters, U.S.-Fr.*, Art. 9(2), S.Treaty Doc. 106-17 ("The procedures specified in this paragraph and outlined in the request shall be carried out insofar as they are not contrary to the fundamental principles of a judicial proceeding in the Requested State. The Requested State, if the Requesting State requests, shall: (a) take the testimony of witnesses or experts under oath ... ; (b) allow a confrontation between a defendant, together with counsel, and a witness or expert whose testimony or evidence is taken for use against the defendant in a criminal prosecution in the Requesting State; (c) ask questions submitted by the Requesting State, including questions proposed by authorities of the Requesting State present at the execution of the request; (d) record or allow to be recorded the testimony, questioning, or confrontation; and (e) produce or allow to be produced a verbatim transcript of the proceeding in which the testimony, questioning, or confrontation occurs").

217 "Hearsay is not admissible except as provided by these rules and by other rules prescribed by the Supreme Court pursuant to statutory authority or by Act of Congress," F.R.Evid. Rule 802. "'Hearsay' is a statement, other than one made by the declarant while testifying at the trial or hearing, offered in evidence to prove the truth of the matter asserted," F.R.Evid. Rule 801(c).

218 "The following are not excluded by the hearsay rule if the declarant is unavailable as a witness: (1) Testimony given as a witness ... in a deposition taken in compliance with law in the course of the same or another proceeding, if the party against whom the testimony is now offered ... had an opportunity and similar motive to develop the testimony by direct, cross, or redirect examination," F.R.Evid. Rule 804(b)(2).

219 *United States v. Medjuck*, 156 F.3d 916, 921 (9th Cir. 1998); *United States v. McKeeve*, 131 F.3d 1, 10 (1st Cir. 1997); *United States v. Kelly*, 892 F.2d 255, 261-62 (3d Cir. 1990).

220 *United States v. McKeeve*, 131 F.3d 1, 9 (1st Cir. 1997); *United States v. Drogoul*, 1 F.3d 1546, 1552 (11th Cir. 1993); *United States v. Kelly*, 892 F.2d 255, 261 (3d Cir. 1989); *United States v. Salim*, 855 F.2d 944, 954-55 (2d Cir. 1988).

221 *United States v. Medjuck*, 156 F.3d 916, 920-21 (9th Cir. 1998).

222 497 U.S. 836, 848 (1990).

223 448 U.S. 56, 66 (1980).

224 541 U.S. 36, 68 (2004) ("Where nontestimonial hearsay is at issue, it is wholly consistent with the Framers' design to afford the states flexibility in their development of hearsay law – as does *Roberts*, and as would an approach that exempted such statements from confrontation

clause scrutiny altogether. Where testimonial evidence is at issue, however, the Sixth Amendment demands what the common law required: unavailability and a prior opportunity for cross-examination").

225 *United States v. Yates*, 438 F.3d 1307, 1316 (11th Cir. 2006).

226 *United States v. Abu Ali*, 528 F.3d 210, 240-42 (4th Cir. 2008).

227 *United States v. Yates*, 438 F.3d 1307, 1316 (11th Cir. 2006) (emphasis added) ("The government's interest in presenting the fact-finding with crucial evidence is, of course, an important public policy. We hold , however, that, under the circumstances of this case (*which include the availability of a Rule 15 deposition*) , the prosecutor's need for the video conference testimony to make a case and to expeditiously resolve it are not the type of public policies that are important enough to outweigh the defendants' rights to confront their accusers face-to-face").

228 *United States v. Abu Ali*, 528 F.3d at 240-42. The Fourth Circuit distinguished *Yates* on the grounds that there the lower court had not considered alternative procedures under which face to face confrontation might have been possible and that there the crimes of conviction were different in kind and degree ("Whatever the merits in *Yates*, the defendants there were charged with mail fraud, conspiracy to commit money laundering, and drug-related offenses, crimes different in both kind and degree from those implicating the national security interests here [(conspiracy commit terrorist attacks on the United States)]," *id.* at 242 n.12.

229 E.g., *In re Terrorist Bombings of U.S. Embassies*, 552 F.3d 93, 118 n.24 (2d Cir. 2008); *United States v. Abu Ali*, 528 F.3d at 257-58; see also, *United States v. el-Mezain*, 664 F.3d 467, 518-19 (5th Cir. 2011)(involving interception of communication in this country under the Foreign Intelligence Surveillance Act).

230 *United States v. Moussaoui*, 382 F.3d 453, 470 (4th Cir. 2004).

231 *United States v. Abu Ali*, 528 F.3d 210, 254 (4th Cir. 2008).

232 18 U.S.C. App. III, 1-16.

233 See generally, CRS Report R41742, *Protecting Classified Information and the Rights of Criminal Defendants: The Classified Information Procedures Act*, by Edward C. Liu and Todd Garvey.

234 *United States v. Abu Ali*, 528 F.3d at 254.

235 "Under §3505, a foreign certification serves to authenticate the foreign records, and thus dispenses with the necessity of calling a live witness to establish authentication," *United States v. Hagege*, 437 F.3d 943, 957 (9th Cir. 2006).

236 "In a criminal proceeding in a court of the United States, a foreign record of regularly conducted activity, or a copy of such record, shall not be excluded as evidence by the hearsay rule if a foreign certification attests that – (A) such record was made, at or near the time of the occurrence of the matters set forth, by (or from information transmitted by) a person with knowledge of those matters; (B) such record was kept in the course of a regularly conducted business activity; (C) the business activity made such a record as a regular practice; and (D) if such record is not the original, such record is a duplicate of the original [–] unless the source of information or the method or circumstances of preparation indicate [a] lack of trustworthiness," 18 U.S.C. 3505(a)(1).

237 "A foreign certification under this section shall authenticate such record or duplicate," 18 U.S.C. 3505(a)(2). "Foreign certification" is "a written declaration made and signed in a foreign country by the custodian of a foreign record of regularly conducted activity or another qualified person that, if falsely made, would subject the maker to criminal penalty under the laws of that country," 18 U.S.C. 3505(c)(2).

238 "At the arraignment or as soon after the arraignment as practicable, a party intending to offer in evidence under this section a foreign record of regularly conducted activity shall provide written notice of that intention to each other party. A motion opposing admission in evidence of such record shall be made by the opposing party and determined by the court before trial. Failure by a party to file such motion before trial shall constitute a waiver of

objection to such record or duplicate, but the court for cause shown may grant relief from the waiver," 18 U.S.C. 3505(b).

239 *United States v. Newell*, 239 F.3d 917, 921 (7th Cir. 2001); *United States v. Garcia Abrego*, 141 F.3d 142, 176-78 (5th Cir. 1998). The court expressed "no opinion as to whether a showing of prejudice resulting from untimely notice of an intent to offer foreign records could eliminate §3505 as a potential pathway for admissibility of foreign business records," 141 F.3d at 178 n. 26.

240 *United States v. Doyle*, 130 F.3d 523, 546 (2d Cir. 1997).

241 *United States v. Garcia Abrego*, 141 F.3d 142, 178-79 (5th Cir. 1998); *United States v. Ross*, 33 F.3d 1507, 1517 (11th Cir. 1994); *United States v. Sturman*, 951 F.2d 1466, 1490 (6th Cir. 1991); *United States v. Miller*, 830 F.2d 1073, 1078 (9th Cir. 1987).

242 541 U.S. 36, 68 (2004) ("Where nontestimonial hearsay is at issue, it is wholly consistent with the Framers' design to afford the states flexibility in their development of hearsay law – as does *Roberts*, and as would an approach that exempted such statements from confrontation clause scrutiny altogether. Where testimonial evidence is at issue, however, the Sixth Amendment demands what the common law required: unavailability and a prior opportunity for cross-examination").

243 541 U.S. at 56.

244 *United States v. Bansal*, 663 F.3d 634, (3d Cir. 2011)("[T]he Supreme Court has indicated that business records are almost never 'testimonial' for Confrontation Clauses purposes, see *Melendez-Dias v. Massachusetts*, 129 S.Ct. 2527, 2539-2540 ... [and] the statements in the records here were made for the purpose of documenting business activity, like car sales and account balances, and not for providing evidence to law enforcement or a jury"); *United States v. Hagege*, 437 F.3d 943, 957-58 (9th Cir. 2006); accord *United States v. Qualls*, 553 F.Supp.2d 241, 244-45 (E.D.N.Y. 2008).

In: Extraterritorial Application ...
Editors: D. Garcia and G. Coleman

ISBN 978-1-62081-445-1

Chapter 2

CIVILIAN EXTRATERRITORIAL JURISDICTION ACT: FEDERAL CONTRACTOR CRIMINAL LIABILITY OVERSEAS*

Charles Doyle

SUMMARY

The United States government uses hundreds of thousands of civilian contractors and employees overseas. They and their dependants are often subject to local prosecution for the crimes they commit abroad. Whether by agreement, practice, or circumstance—sometimes they are not. The Military Extraterritorial Jurisdiction Act (MEJA) permits federal prosecution of certain crimes committed abroad by Defense Department civilian employees, contractors, or their dependants. The Civilian Extraterritorial Jurisdiction Act (CEJA; H.R. 2136) (Representative Price of North Carolina) and S. 1145 (Senator Leahy) would permit federal prosecution for certain crimes committed abroad by the civilian employees, dependants, or contractors of other federal agencies.

The bills would supplement rather than replace MEJA or other provisions of federal extraterritorial jurisdiction. The crimes covered would include various federal violent, corruption, and trafficking offenses. The Attorney

* This is an edited, reformatted and augmented version of a Congressional Research Service publication, CRS Report for Congress R42358, prepared for Members and Committees of Congress, from www.crs.gov, dated February 15, 2012.

General would be responsible to ensure the availability of personnel and other resources necessary for investigation and prosecution of such offenses.

Otherwise applicable statutes of limitation would be suspended during the absence of a suspect from the United States. Prosecutors would be afforded the additional option of trying cases under CEJA in the district in which the employing or contracting agency maintained its headquarters.

INTRODUCTION

The United States government utilizes the services of hundreds of thousands of employees and contractors overseas.[1] In some instances, US agreements with the host nation preclude local prosecution of the crimes they commit.[2] Federal law, as now written, does not always permit federal prosecution.[3] The Civilian Extraterritorial Jurisdiction Act (H.R. 2136 and S. 1145) would fill some of the perceived gaps. The House bill, introduced by Representative Price, and the Senate bill, introduced by Senator Leahy and approved with amendments by the Senate Judiciary Committee, are very similar but not identical. They each address objections voiced concerning comparable proposals passed by the House during the 110th Congress.

BACKGROUND

Criminal law is usually territorial. In some instances, however, a nation's interests and responsibilities permit the extraterritorial application of its law to matters beyond its borders.4 So it is with the crimes of those associated with the United States government's activities overseas. The Uniform States Code of Military Justice (UCMJ) applies to crimes committed by members of the United States Armed Forces, wherever they may be.5 The Military Extraterritorial Jurisdiction Act (MEJA) applies to certain felonies committed by those employed by or accompanying the Armed Forces abroad.[6] The USA PATRIOT Act amended the federal criminal code to make portions of it applicable to crimes committed by Americans within federal facilities and residences overseas.[7] Legislation in 2006 established extraterritorial jurisdiction over Mann Act and human trafficking offenses, when committed by those employed by or accompanying the federal government overseas.[8]

Events in Iraq in 2007 raised questions about whether these provisions are sufficient to apply to allegations of misconduct by contractors employed by agencies other than the Department of Defense.[9] The House responded with passage of H.R. 2740 (110th Congress), which, among other things, would have made MEJA applicable to employees of any contractor for "any department or agency of the United States, where the work under such contract is carried out in an area, or in close proximity to an area (as designated by the Department of Defense), where the Armed Forces is conducting a contingency operation."[10]

At the time, the Administration objected that the bill

- was vague;[11]
- would afford a sweeping number of offenses extraterritorial application;[12]
- would impermissibly direct FBI overseas activities;[13] and
- would burden the Defense Department with implementation responsibilities.[14]

The Senate took no action on the House-passed bill in the 110th Congress. Modified proposals were reintroduced in the 111th Congress. Witnesses at congressional hearings discussed the matter, but no further legislative activity occurred.[15]

H.R. 2136 AND S. 1145 (112TH CONGRESS)

Constitutional Considerations

"[T]he Federal 'Government is acknowledged by all to be one of enumerated powers,' which means that 'every law enacted by Congress must be based on one or more of' those powers."[16] Nevertheless, the Constitution is particularly generous in the powers which it grants the federal government, and consequently the Congress, with regard to matters overseas. It designates the President commander in chief of the armed forces of the United States and empowers Congress to make rules for their government and regulation.[17] It vests in the President the power to receive foreign ambassadors, and with the advice and consent of the Senate, to make treaties and appoint ambassadors.[18] It grants Congress an array of enumerated powers that includes the power to define and punish felonies on the high seas and contrary to the law of nations, to regulate commerce with foreign nations, and to pass laws to carry into effect any of the powers which the Constitution vests in it, in the President, in the federal government, or in any federal officer or department.[19] Such limitations as may exist must be found in the scope of the enumerated powers themselves or in constitutional prohibitions—either explicit restrictions, such the ban on ex post facto laws, or implicit restrictions, such as those that follow from the due process clause.

Curtiss-Wright provides some support for the proposition that where Congress's enumerated powers are wanting, extraterritorial jurisdiction may be based on sovereignty.[20] Its exercise of that power is limited by law of nations as well as by due process.[21]

MEJA has recently withstood constitutional challenges which argued that it exceeded Congress's enumerated powers.[22] In *Green*, the Sixth Circuit also rejected the argument that expanding the circumstances under which executive branch officials might enforce a criminal statute constituted violation of a separation of powers principles.[23] In the absence of encroachment of one branch upon the powers of another the Court could find no separation of powers infirmity.[24] Green argued in addition that trying him under MEJA while trying his coconspirators under the UCMJ denied him equal protection of the law. Green who had been discharged and his coconspirators who had not were not similarly situated. Green's equal protection argument thus turned upon evidence of purely arbitrary or malicious official conduct, neither of which he had shown, the court found.[25] Nor could the court find that Green's discharge and subsequent prosecution under MEJA so shocked the conscience of the court as to constitute a violation of due process.[26]

The district court in *Williams* greeted the argument that MEJA exceeded Congress's enumerated powers with the assertion that, "there is no constitutional bar to the extraterritorial application of penal laws."[27] The court then declared that, "[b]efore finding the MEJA to be a proper exercise of Congress' extraterritorial power, however, the Court must 'consider whether [giving extraterritorial effect to the penal statute] would violate general principles of international law.'"[28] It is unclear whether the court felt this consideration was necessary (1) to confirm the intent of Congress; (2) to bring the statute within the reach of Congress's power as sovereign or under Article I, §8, cl. 10, to define and punish offenses under the law of nations; or (3) to a guide a due process analysis. As for confirming congressional intent, the cases which the court cites address the question of whether a statute, silent as to its extraterritorial application, was intended to apply overseas.[29] The overseas application of MEJA, however, is explicit and so reference to international law to discern congressional intent seems unnecessary.

The court initially suggested that it might view the principles of international law as indicative of the scope of Congress's sovereign power or its power to define and punish offenses under the law of nations pursuant to Article I, §8, cl. 10. It described the pertinent principles of international law as the "law of nations," "[t]he law of nations permits the exercise of criminal jurisdiction by a nation under five general principles: (1) the objective territorial, (2) the national, (3) the protective, (4) the universal, and (5) the passive personality."[30] Yet, the court went on to find application of MEJA in the case before it consistent with each of the five principles—other than universal principle—the one principle that it characterized as embodying the law of nations.[31]

Were the timing different, the district court might have been mindful of the Eleventh Circuit's observation that, "[i]n determining whether an extraterritorial law comports with due process, appellate courts often consult international law principles."[32] In any event, the court found "that the MEJA is a proper application of Congress's extraterritorial power, ... [b]ecause Congress clearly intended the MEJA to be applied extraterritorially, and because such extraterritorial application of the MEJA would not offend international law."[33]

The House Judiciary Committee report on MEJA indicates that constitutional authority to enact its provisions may be found in: Article I, section 8, clauses 10 ["To define and punish ... Offenses against the Law of Nations"], 14 ["To make Rules for the Government and Regulation of the land and naval Forces"], 16 ["To provide ... for governing such Part of [the militia] as may be employed in the Service of the United States"], and 18 ["To make all Laws ... necessary and proper for carrying into Execution the foregoing Powers, and all other Powers vested by this Constitution in [the President] ... ").[34]

Congress may rely upon a wider range of its enumerated powers to enact the bills' proposals, based on the legislative authority for (1) the contracts or employment of those covered by the proposals, (2) the offenses covered by the proposals, or (3) the location of the offenses. The Constitutional Authority Statement for H.R. 2136 identifies three constitutional justifications: the power to tax and spend for the common defense and general welfare,[35] the power to define and punish offenses against the law of nations,[36] and the power "to legislate with respect to matters outside US boundaries ... based on national sovereignty in foreign affairs."[37]

Who

The House and Senate bills in the 112th Congress supplement rather than amend MEJA. They would establish a new section 3272 outlawing conduct outside the United States by anyone "employed by or accompanying any department or agency of the United States other than the Department of Defense," when the conduct would be criminal if committed within the United States or within its special maritime and territorial jurisdiction.[38] The bills identify those "employed by" or "accompanying" as employees, contractors, subcontractors, grantees, subgrantee as well as their dependants, family members, and members of their households.[39] They would exclude nationals and ordinary residents of the host country and encompass only employees, contractors, and their attendants whose presence abroad is attributable to support of a federal, non-Defense Department program, project, or activity.[40]

The definitions are comparable to those found in MEJA.[41] MEJA, however, does not specifically mention grantees, family members or household members.[42] The bills do.[43] The bills would also reach the crimes of a wider range of non-Defense Department employees, contractors, and attendants than MEJA. MEJA reaches the crimes of a few. Its limited scope extends to various crimes committed by the employees and contractors of "any other Federal agency, or any provisional authority, to the extent such employment relates to supporting the mission of the Department of Defense overseas."[44] An incident in Iraq triggered concerns that contractors assigned to such tasks as traffic control for a State Department motorcade may not be engaged in activities relate "to supporting the mission the Department of Defense."[45]

Where MEJA looks to crimes committed by those engaged in activities relating to a Defense Department mission, the bills would look to crimes committed by those engaged in activities relating to "a program, project, or activity for a department or agency of the United States other than the Defense Department."[46]

The bills would not repeal or amend MEJA's coverage of non-Defense Department employees, contractors, and dependants.[47] Thus, prosecutors would be free to proceed under either MEJA or the bill's proposed section, in cases involving employees, dependants, or contractors of such civilian agencies whose activities related to support of a Defense Department mission.

The bills appear limited to the crimes of executive branch employees, contractors, and those accompanying them, because the bills refer to individuals associated with "any department or agency of the United States other than the Department of Defense." As used in the criminal code, that term "department or agency of the United States" is usually understood not to apply to the legislative and judicial branches of government, unless the context suggests otherwise.[48]

What Crimes

MEJA describes the crimes to which it applies generically: "an offense punishable by imprisonment for more than 1 year if the conduct had been engaged in within the special maritime and territorial jurisdiction of the United States."[49] In the 110th Congress, OMB considered comparable coverage for non-Defense Department contractors too sweeping.[50] Perhaps with this in mind, the bills provide a list of specific offenses to which its extraterritorial provisions would apply. The list includes drug trafficking, terrorism offenses, assault, murder, and most of the other common law offenses that would be subject to federal prosecution had they occurred within the United States or its special maritime or territorial jurisdiction.[51] The list is arguably as extensive as the list of offenses covered by MEJA.[52]

Past and present Administrations have sought an exception for United States intelligence activities abroad.[53] The two bills would create such an exception, although in slightly differently terms. The House bill would exempt authorized intelligence activities *conducted* in accordance with applicable law; the Senate bill would exempt authorized intelligence activities *authorized* in accordance with applicable law.[54] Both bills disclaim any intent to curtail other grants of extraterritorial jurisdiction or to negate any authority of responsibilities of the various chiefs of mission.[55]

Implementation

MEJA has a number of procedural provisions designed to minimize the adverse impact of investigating and prosecuting those closely associated with military activities. More precisely, out of deference to the Posse Comitatus Act, MEJA explicitly authorizes overseas US military law enforcement personnel to arrest those charged with MEJA violations.[56] Out of deference to groups representing the interests of overseas employees, MEJA contains several provisions designed to avoid an arbitrary return to the United States to face unfounded charges.[57] Those arrested for federal criminal offenses outside the United States must be brought before a federal magistrate "without unnecessary delay,"[58] although the initial appearance may be conducted by telephone or videoconference.[59] There, the magistrate may appoint military counsel to represent indigent defendants, and may dismiss the charges for want of probable cause or upon a finding of probable cause set bail.[60] The magistrate may also order the accused returned to the States; otherwise an accused may not be removed except for military necessity.[61]

The bills would establish no comparable provisions. However, they would vest the Attorney General, in consultation with the Director of National Intelligences and the Secretaries of State and Defense, with authority to promulgate regulations governing arrest, detention, delivery, and removal of individuals under the proposals.[62] Under the House bill, the regulations would include an allocation of responsibility for the investigation of cases that involve a killing, serious bodily injury, property damage in excess of $10,000, or the discharge of a firearm.[63] The Senate bill has no comparable provisions.

Earlier proposals would have amended MEJA. OMB objected that this might impose unwarranted investigative burdens upon the Defense Department.[64] The bills would shift the burden to the Attorney General, to be shared by the departments and agencies with covered employees, contractors, and grantees. The Attorney General would be directed to assign sufficient personnel and resources to investigate possible overseas violation of the offenses covered by the bills.[65] He would be empowered to request assistance to conduct such investigations from the agencies with employees and contractors abroad, including the Departments of Defense and State.[66]

The Attorney General would also be obligated to report to Congress annually for six years on activities under the proposals and on any recommendations for related administrative or legislative adjustments, again after conferring with the Secretaries of State and Defense.[67]

Statute of Limitations

The bills would adjust the applicable statute of limitations.[68] The statute of limitations refers to the statutory period within which a prosecution must be commenced. It begins with the commission of the offense.[69] A prosecution begins for purposes of the statute of limitations with the filing or an indictment or information.[70]

"The purpose of a statute of limitations is to limit exposure to criminal prosecution to a certain fixed period of time following the occurrence of those acts the legislature has decided to punish by criminal sanctions. Such a limitation is designed to protect individuals from having to defend themselves against charges when the basic facts may have become obscured by the passage of time and to minimize the danger of official punishment because of acts in the far-distant past. Such a time limit may also have the salutary effect of encouraging law enforcement officials promptly to investigate suspected criminal activity." [71]

The statute of limitations for most federal crimes is five years.[72] A few individual offenses have longer statutes of limitations. Arson, for instance, has a 10-year statute of limitations.[73]

Capital offenses or certain terrorism and sex offenses are not subject to any period of limitation and may be prosecuted at any time.[74] Under some circumstances, the applicable statute of limitations will be suspended. For example, the limitation governing prosecution of fraud against the United States is suspended during wartime,[75] and during any period when the suspect was in flight.[76]

Because the statute of limitations runs from the commission of the crime to indictment, it operates as an investigation time table. Given the difficulties often associated with an overseas investigation, proposals to adjust the statute of limitations in such cases come as no surprise. The bills each propose a suspension of any applicable statute of limitations during the period a suspect is abroad.[77]

The House proposal would apply to offenses for which it would provide extraterritorial jurisdiction as well as to offenses under 18 USC. 3271 which establishes such jurisdiction of certain human trafficking offenses: "The statute of limitations for an offense involving a violation of section 3271 or 3272 shall be computed without regard to any time the alleged offender is outside the United States."

The Senate proposal has no reference to the trafficking section, but includes a cross reference to the fugitive provisions of 18 USC. 3290: "The time during which a person who has committed an offense constituting a violation of section 3272 of this title is outside the United States, or is a fugitive from justice within the meaning of section 3290 of this title, shall not be take as any part of the time limited by law for commencement of prosecution of the offense."

Under either proposal, the statute of limitations would only run while the suspect is in the United States. This might have the effect of eliminating the statute of limitations for overseas employees and contractors who are foreign nationals with no particular reason to come to the United States.

Venue

The Constitution insists that federal crimes be tried in the state and district in which they were committed, but affords Congress considerable latitude to decree where federal crimes committed overseas may be tried.[78] Under existing law, a defendant may be tried for an overseas crime in the district in which he is first arrested or brought. If indicted prior to arrest, he may be tried in the district in which he last resided or in the District of Columbia when his last place of residence in the United States is unknown.[79]

"[T]his statute permits the government to handpick its forum in the case of a person first found overseas, by picking the district to which it will return him;"[80] less so in the case of a person residing in the United States when the government is first ready to make an arrest or seek an indictment.

Both bills would afford the government an additional venue option. They would permit trial in the district in which the employing or contracting agency maintains its headquarters.[81] The option would be available for the offenses over which the bills establish extraterritorial jurisdiction and for human trafficking and sex travel offenses over which in extraterritorial jurisdiction exists by virtue of 18 USC. 3271.[82] The Senate bill would also afford the government the option in MEJA cases.[83]

When exercised, the option would operate to the disadvantage of the accused in some instances. Defendants, who resided in a district other than one in which their employing or contracting agency maintained its headquarters, could face the additional expense and inconvenience of trial in a remote location and the prospective of more onerous bail conditions or pre-trial detention.[84]

On the other hand, the option might operate to enhance the prospect of a plea agreement, thus sparing the government the expense of a trial. It might also operate to the greater convenience of witnesses assigned, or who might be assigned, to duties in the headquarters of the employing or contracting agency.

ATTACHMENT 1

Extraterritorial Offenses under H.R. 2136 and S. 1145: Proposed 18 USC. 3272

(a) Whoever, while employed by or accompanying any department or agency of the United States other than the Department of Defense, knowingly engages in conduct (or conspires or attempts to engage in conduct) outside the United States that would constitute an offense enumerated in subsection (c) had the conduct been engaged in within the United States or within the special maritime and territorial jurisdiction of the United States shall be punished as provided for that offense... .

(c) The offenses covered by subsection (a) are the following:

1) Any offense under chapter 5 (arson) of this title [18 USC. 81 (arson within the special maritime and territorial jurisdiction)].
2) Any offense under section 111 (assaulting, resisting, or impeding certain officers or employees), 113 (assault within maritime and territorial jurisdiction), or 114 (maiming within maritime and territorial jurisdiction) of this title, but only if the offense is subject to a maximum sentence of imprisonment of one year or more.
3) Any offense under section 201 (bribery of public officials and witnesses) of this title.
4) Any offense under section 499 (military, naval, or official passes) of this title.
5) Any offense under section 701 (official badges, identification cards, and other insignia), 702 (uniform of armed forces and Public Health Service), 703 (uniform of friendly nation), or 704 (military medals or decorations) of this title.
6) Any offense under chapter 41 (extortion and threats) of this title [18 USC. 871 (threats against the President), 872 (extortion by federal employees involving more than $1,000), 874 (kickbacks from public works employees), 875 (extortionate wire communications involving threats to kidnap or inflict bodily injury), 876 (mailing extortionate threats to kidnap or inflict bodily injury), 877 (mailing extortionate threats to kidnap or inflict bodily injury to the United States from overseas), 878 (extortionate threats to kidnap or inflict bodily injury against internationally protected persons), 879 (threats against former Presidents)], but only if the offense is subject to a maximum sentence of imprisonment of three years or more.
7) Any offense under chapter 42 (extortionate credit transactions) of this title [18 USC. 892, 893 (making or financing such transactions)] of this title.
8) Any offense under section 924(c) (use of firearm in violent or drug trafficking crime) or 924(o) (conspiracy to violate section 924(c)) of this title.

9) Any offense under chapter 50A (genocide) of this title.
10) Any offense under section 1111 (murder), 1112 (manslaughter), 1113 (attempt to commit murder or manslaughter), 1114 (protection of officers and employees of the United States), 1116 (murder or manslaughter of foreign officials, official guests, or internationally protected persons), 1117 (conspiracy to commit murder), or 1119 (foreign murder of United States nationals) of this title.
11) Any offense under chapter 55 (kidnapping) of this title [18 USC. 1201 (kidnapping), 1202 (receipt of ransom money), 1203 (hostage taking), 1204 (international parental kidnapping)].
12) Any offense under section 1503 (influencing or injuring officer or juror generally), 1505 (obstruction of proceedings before departments, agencies, and committees), 1510 (obstruction of criminal investigations), 1512 (tampering with a witness, victim, or informant), or 1513 (retaliating against a witness, victim, or an informant) of this title.
13) Any offense under section 1951 (interference with commerce by threats or violence), 1952 (interstate and foreign travel or transportation in aid of racketeering enterprises), 1956 (laundering of monetary instruments), 1957 (engaging in monetary transactions in property derived from specified unlawful activity), 1958 (use of interstate commerce facilities in the commission of murder for hire), or 1959 (violent crimes in aid of racketeering activity) of this title.
14) Any offense under section 2111 (robbery or burglary within special maritime and territorial jurisdiction) of this title.
15) Any offense under chapter 109A (sexual abuse) of this title [18 USC. 2241 (aggravated sexual abuse), 2242 (sexual abuse), 2243 (sexual abuse of a minor or ward), 2244 (abusive sexual contact)].
16) Any offense under chapter 113B (terrorism) of this title [18 USC. 2332 (violence against Americans overseas), 2332a (use of weapons of mass destruction), 2332b(multinational terrorism), 2332d (financial transactions with nations supporting terrorism), 2332f (bombing public facilities), 2332g (possession of anti-aircraft missiles), 2332h (possession of radiological dispersal device), 2339 (harboring terrorists), 2339A (providing material support for terrorist offenses), 2339B (providing material support for terrorist organizations), 2339C (financing terrorism), 2339D (receipt of training from terrorist organizations)].
17) Any offense under chapter 113C (torture) of this title.

18) Any offense under chapter 115 (treason, sedition, and subversive activities) of this title [18 USC. 2381 (treason), 2382 (misprision of treason), 2383 (rebellion or insurrection), 2384 (seditious conspiracy), 2385 (advocating overthrow of the government), 2386 (registration of foreign political or military organizations), 2387 (activity adversely affecting the armed forces), 2388 (activity adversely affecting the armed forces during wartime), 2389 (recruiting for services against the United States), 2390 (enlistment to serve against the United States)].
19) Any offense under section 2442 (child soldiers) of this title.
20) Any offense under section 401 (manufacture, distribution, or possession with intent to distribute a controlled substance) or 408 (continuing criminal enterprise) of the Controlled Substances Act (21 USC. 841, 848), or under section 1002 (importation of controlled substances), 1003 (exportation of controlled substances), or 1010 (import or export of a controlled substance) of the Controlled Substances Import and Export Act (21 USC. 952, 953, 960), but only if the offense is subject to a maximum sentence of imprisonment of 20 years or more.

ATTACHMENT 2

Extraterritorial Offenses under MEJA (Special Maritime and Territorial Jurisdiction)

8 USC. 1375a(d)(3) (informed consent violations by international marriage brokers) *15 USC. 1175* (manufacture or possession of gambling devices) *15 USC. 1243* (manufacture or possession of switchblade knives)

15 USC. 1245 (manufacture or possession of ballistic knives)

16 USC. 3372(a)(3) (possession of illegally taken fish or wildlife)

18 USC. 32 (destruction of aircraft)

18 USC. 81 (arson)

18 USC. 113 (assault)

18 USC. 114 (maiming)

18 USC. 115 (violence against federal officials, former officials and members of their families)

18 USC. 117 (domestic assault by an habitual offender)

18 USC. 118 (interference with certain protective functions [State Department & diplomatic security])
18 USC. 249 (hate crimes)
18 USC. 546 (smuggling goods into a foreign country from an American vessel)
18 USC. 661 (theft)
18 USC. 662 (receipt of stolen property)
18 USC. 831 (threats, theft, or unlawful possession of nuclear material or attempting or conspiring to do so)
18 USC. 1025 (false pretenses)
18 USC. 1081 - 1083 (gambling ships)
18 USC. 1111 (murder)
18 USC. 1112 (manslaughter)
18 USC. 1113 (attempted murder or manslaughter)
18 USC. 1115 (misconduct or neglect by ship officers)
18 USC. 1201 (kidnaping)
18 USC. 1363 (malicious mischief)
18 USC. 1460 (sale or possession with intent to sell obscene material)
18 USC. 1466A (obscene visual representation of sexual abuse of children)
18 USC. 1587 (captain of a slave vessel with slaves aboard)
18 USC. 1591(sex trafficking of children)
18 USC. 1656 (piratical conversion of vessel by captain, officer or crew member)
18 USC. 1658 (plundering a ship in distress)
18 USC. 1659 (attack upon a vessel with intent to plunder)
18 USC. 1654 (Americans arming or serving on privateers outside the United States to be used against the United States or Americans)
18 USC. 1801 (video voyeurism)
18 USC. 1957 (prohibited monetary transactions) *18 USC. 2111* (robbery)
18 USC. 2191 (cruelty to seamen)
18 USC. 2192 (incite to revolt or mutiny) *18 USC. 2193* (revolt or mutiny by seamen)
18 USC. 2194 (shanghaiing sailors)
18 USC. 2195 (abandonment of sailors overseas)
18 USC. 2196 (drunkenness of seamen)
18 USC. 2197 (misuse of documents associated vessels)
18 USC. 2198 (seduction of a female passenger)
18 USC. 2199 (stowaways)
18 USC. 2241 (aggravated sexual abuse)

18 USC. 2242 (sexual abuse)
18 USC. 2243 (sexual abuse of a minor or ward)
18 USC. 2244 (abusive sexual contact)
18 USC. 2252(a) (sale or possession of material involving sexual exploitation of children)
18 USC. 2252A(a) (sale or possession of child pornography)
18 USC. 2261 (interstate domestic violence)
18 USC. 2261A (stalking)
18 USC. 2262 (interstate violation of a protective order)
18 USC. 2271-2279 (destruction of ships)
18 USC. 2283 (transportation of explosives, biological, chemical, radioactive or nuclear materials for terrorist purposes on the high seas or aboard a US vessel or in US waters)
18 USC. 2284 (transportation of a terrorist on the high seas or aboard a US vessel or in US waters) *18 USC. 2318* (transporting counterfeit phonorecord labels, copies of computer programs or documentation, or copies of motion pictures or other audio visual works)
18 USC. 2332b (acts of terrorism transcending national boundaries)
18 USC. 2388 (war-time activities affecting armed forces)
18 USC. 2422(b) (causing a minor to engage in prostitution or other sexual acts)
18 USC. 2425 (transmission of information about a minor)
18 USC. 3261(offenses committed by members of the United States armed forces or individuals accompanying or employed by the United States armed forces overseas)
46 USC. 70503 (maritime drug law enforcement)
46 USC. 70508 (operation of stateless submersible vessels)
48 USC. 1912 (offenses committed on United States defense sites in the Marshall Islands or Federated States of Micronesia)
48 USC.1934 (offenses committed on United States defense sites in Palau)
49 USC. 46502(a) (air piracy or attempted air piracy)
49 USC. 46504 (interference with flight crew or attendants within the special aircraft jurisdiction of the United States)
49 USC. 46506 (assaults, maiming, theft, receipt of stolen property, murder, manslaughter, attempted murder or manslaughter, robbery, or sexual abuse)

End Notes

[1] At one point, the Defense Department, State Department and USAID employed over 200,000 contractor personnel in Iraq and Afghanistan alone, Government Accountability Office, *Contingency Contracting: DOD, State, and USAID Contracts and Contractor Personnel in Iraq and Afghanistan: Report to Congressional Committees*, 6-7 (GAO-09-19) (Oct. 2008); see also, Williams, *The Case for Overseas Article III Courts: The Blackwater Effect and Criminal Accountability in the Age of Privatization*, 44 UNIVERSITY OF MICHIGAN JOURNAL OF LAW REFORM 45, 47 (2010)("[W]e can conservatively estimate that nearly 500,000 civilian employees, dependents, and contractors of the US government currently enjoy de facto immunity form meaningful criminal accountability.... Of this number, approximately 340,000 are Americans ... ").

[2] See generally, CRS Report RL34531, *Status of Forces Agreement (SOFA): What Is It, and How Has It Been Utilized?*, by R. Chuck Mason.

[3] *Holding Criminals Accountable: Extending Criminal Jurisdiction for Government Contractors and Employees Abroad: Hearing Before the Senate Comm. on the Judiciary*, 112th Cong., 1st sess. (2011)(statement of Ass't Att'y Gen. Lanny A. Breuer)("Since MEJA's passage in 2000, we have aggressively enforced MEJA against Department of Defense employees, contractors, and individuals accompanying them. We have also investigated a number of matters involving non-Department of Defense persons when we can establish that their employment relates to supporting the mission of the department of Defense overseas or where we had extra-territorial jurisdiction under other statutes. However, under the current law, certain US Government employees can commit crimes overseas without been prosecuted").

[4] See generally, *The Extraterritorial Application of American Criminal Law*, CRS Rept. 94-166.

[5] 10 USC. 802. Until 2007, the UCMJ applied to civilians "in time of war" with respect to those "serving with or accompanying an armed force in the field," 10 USC. 802(a)(10)(2006 ed.). The limitation apparently reflected the fact that the Supreme Court had been reluctant to allow application of military law to civilians, *United States ex rel. Toth v. Quarles*, 350 US 11, 23 (1955)(holding that an airman, charged with a murder committed while he was serving with the Air Force, could not constitutionally be tried by court martial after his discharge); *Reid v. Covert*, 354 US1, 39-40, 64, 77-8 (1957)(holding that military dependents, accompanying the armed forces overseas and charged with murdering their husbands, could not be tried by courts martial); *Kinsella v. United States ex rel. Singleton*, 361 US 234, 249 (1960)(holding such a dependent, charged the noncapital killing of her husband, could not tried by court martial). In 2007, Congress enlarged the provision to apply to those serving with or accompanying an armed force in the field, "in time of declared war or a contingency operation," P.L. 109-364, §552, Stat. (2007), codified at 10 USC. 802(a)(10).

[6] 18 USC. 3261.

[7] 18 USC. 7(9).

[8] 18 USC. 3271 applies to violations of 18 USC. chs. 77 (peonage, slavery, and trafficking in persons) and 117 (transportation for illegal sexual activity).

[9] H.Rept. 110-352 (2007).

[10] H.R. 2740 (110th Cong.), §2(a)(1), reprinted in H.Rept. 110-352, at 2 (2007). The bill passed the House on October 4, 2007, 153 *Cong. Rec.* 26632-639 (2007). The 110th Congress adjourned without Senate action on H.R. 2740.

[11] "First, the jurisdictional scope of criminal prohibitions would depend on vague notions of 'proximity' to potentially poorly defined regions, making unclear the circumstances when those who assist the United States government would be subject to the bill's criminal sanctions and raising significant Due Process concerns. The Administration is very concerned that, if enacted, this bill will give rise to extensive litigation on jurisdictional issues," Office of Management and Budget (OMB), *Statement of Administration Policy: H.R. 2740 – MEJA Expansion and Enforcement Act of 2007* (Oct. 3, 2007), available at www. cq.com/graphics/hotdocs/27131-sapon-hr2740-10307.pdf.

[12] "Second, the bill broadly expands criminal jurisdiction extraterritorially for most felony offenses in the US Code. The Administration is concerned that this sweeping expansion of extraterritorial jurisdiction would create Federal jurisdiction overseas in situations where it would be impossible or unwise to extend it. The bill would have unintended and intolerable consequences for crucial and necessary national security activities and operations," *id.*

[13] "Third, the bill would affirmatively mandate that particular investigative activities of the Federal Bureau of Investigation be conducted overseas. It would upend a time-honored system of responsible law enforcement personnel allocating scarce law enforcement resources to the Nation's greatest needs. By attempting to set statutory requirements to investigate not only reports of fatalities, but also reports that merely raise suspicion of misconduct by personnel, the legislation would intrude on decisions the Constitution reserves to the Executive Branch," *id.*

[14] "Fourth, the bill would place inappropriate and unwarranted burdens on the Department of Defense. In addition to their overriding responsibility to conduct military operations, the Armed Forces would be required to undertake significant duties for the handling and detention of non-DOD contractors covered by the bill. The bill further would obligate DOD – in the middle of ongoing armed conflicts in theaters of war – to support criminal investigations undertaken by the FBI," *id.*

[15] H.R. 4567 (111th Cong.)(Rep. Price); S. 2979 (111th Cong.)(Sen. Leahy).

[16] *United States v. Comstock*, 130 S.Ct. 1949, 1956 (2010), quoting *McCulloch v. Maryland*, 4 Wheat. (17 US) 316, 405 (1819), and *United States v. Morrison*, 529 US 598, 607 (2000), respectively.

[17] US Const. Art. II, §2; Art. I, §8, cl.14.

[18] US Const. Art. II, §3, §2, cl.2.

[19] US Const. Art. I, §8, cls. 10, 3, 18.

[20] *United States v. Curtiss-Wright Export Corp.*, 299 US 304, 315-16, 318 (1936)("The broad statement that the federal government can exercise no powers except those specifically enumerated in the Constitution, and such implied powers as are necessary and proper to carry into effect the enumerated powers, is categorically true only in respect to our internal affairs.... It results that the investment of the federal government with the powers of external sovereignty did not depend upon the affirmative grants of the Constitution").

[21] *Id.* at 318 ("[O]perations of the nation in such [foreign] territory must be governed by treaties, international understandings and compacts, and the principles of international law.... [T]he court recognized, and in each of the cases cited [involving the authority of the United States a sovereign] found, the warrant for its conclusions ... in the law of nations").

[22] *United States v. Green*, 654 F.3d 637 (6th Cir. 2011); *United States v. Williams*, 722 F.Supp. 2d 1313 (M.D.Ga. 2010).

[23] *United States v. Green*, 654 F.3d at 645-50.

[24] *Id.*

[25] *Id.* at 650-52.

[26] *Id.* at 652-53.

[27] *United States v. Williams*, 722 F.Supp.2d at 1317.

[28] *Id.* at 1318, quoting *United States v. MacAllister*, 160 F.3d 1304, 1308 (11th Cir. 1998), and citing *United States Vasquez-Velasco*, 15 F.3d 833, 839 (9th Cir. 1994).

[29] *United States v. MacAllister*, 160 F.3d at 1306 ("This is a question of statutory interpretation"); *United States Vasquez-Velasco*, 15 F.3d at 839 ("In determining whether a given statute should have extraterritorial application in a specific case, courts look to congressional intent").

[30] *United States v. Williams*, 722 F.Supp.2d at 1318.

[31] *Id.* at 1319, 1318 n. 9 (portions of the court's footnote in brackets)("The Court finds that extraterritorial jurisdiction is permitted by all but the 'universal' principle of international law. [... the universality principle permits a State to prosecute an offender of any nationality for an offense committed outside of that State and without contacts to that State, but only for the few, near-unique offenses recognized by the 'civilized nations' as an offense against the 'Law of Nations'").

[32] *United States v. Ibarguen-Mosquera*, 634 F.3d 1370, 1378 (11th Cir. 2011).

[33] *United States v. Williams*, 722 F.Supp.2d at 1319.

[34] H.Rept. 106-778, at 14 (2000).

[35] US Const. Art. I, §1, cl.1.

[36] US Const. Art. I, §8, cl.10.

[37] 157 *Cong. Rec.* H4035 (daily ed. June 3, 2011).

[38] H.R. 2136, §2(a)(3), proposed 18 USC. 3272(a); S. 1145, §2(a)(1)(C), proposed 18 USC. 3272(a).

[39] H.R. 2136, §2(a)(3), proposed 18 USC. 3272(e)(1); S. 1145, §2(a)(1)(C), proposed 18 USC. 3272(d)(1): "The term 'employed by any department or agency of the United States other than the Department of Defense' means – (A) employed as a civilian employee, a contractor (including a subcontractor at any tier), an employee of a contractor (or a subcontractor at any tier), a grantee (including a contractor of a grantee or a subgrantee or subcontractor at any tier), or an employee of a grantee (or a contractor of a grantee or a subgrantee or subcontractor at any tier) of any department or agency of the United States other than the Department of Defense; (B) present or residing outside the United States in connection with such employment; (C) in the case of such a contractor, contractor employee, grantee, or grantee employee, such employment supports a program, project, or activity for a department or agency of the United States; and (D) not a national of or ordinarily resident in the host nation." The text of the definition of "accompanying" appears in the following footnote.

[40] H.R. 2136, §2(a)(3), proposed 18 USC. 3272(e)(2); S. 1145, §2(a)(1)(C), proposed 18 USC. 3272(d)(2): "The term 'accompanying any department or agency of the United States other than the Department of Defense' means – (A) a dependant, family member, or member of household of – (i) a civilian employee of any department or agency of the United States other than the Department of Defense; or (ii) a contractor (including a subcontractor at any tier), an employee of a contractor (or a subcontractor at any tier), a grantee (including a contractor of a grantee or a subgrantee or subcontractor at any tier), or an employee of a grantee (or a contractor of a grantee or a subgrantee or subcontractor at any tier) of any department or agency of the United States other than the Department of Defense, which contractor, contractor employee, grantee, or grantee employee is supporting a program, project, or activity for a department or agency of the United States other than the Department of Defense; (B) residing with such civilian employee, contractor, contractor

employee, grantee, or grantee employee outside the United States; and (C) not a national of or ordinarily resident in the host nation."

[41] See 18 USC. 3267 (MEJA definitions).

[42] The MEJA definitions make no mention of grants or grantees and include only dependants within their definition of "accompanying," 18 USC. 3267(1), (2).

[43] H.R. 2136, §2(a)(3), proposed 18 USC. 3272(e)(1)(A), (2)(A); S. 1145, §2(a)(1)(C), proposed 18 USC. 3272(d)(1)(A), (2)(A).

[44] 18 USC. 3267(1)(A)(i)(II).

[45] 157 Cong. Rec. S3500 (daily ed. June 6, 2011)(remarks of Sen. Leahy)("In September 2007, Blackwater security contractors working for the state Department shot more than 20 unarmed civilians on the streets of Baghdad, killing at least 14 of them.... Efforts to prosecute those responsible for these shootings have been fraught with difficulties, and our ability to hold the wrongdoers in this case accountable remains in doubt"); see also, Indictment at 2, United States v. Slough, Crim. No. CR-08-360 (D.D.C. Dec. 4, 2008)(" ... defendants ... were employed by the Armed Forces outside the United States, as defined in 18 USC. §3267(1), that is: a. The defendants were employees and subcontractors of Blackwater Worldwide, a company contracting with the United States Department of State, who were employed to provide personal security services in the Republic of Iraq, which employment related to supporting the mission of the United States Department of Defense in the Republic of Iraq"); United States v. Slough, 641 F.3d 544, 547 (D.C.Cir. 2011)(internal citations omitted)("On September 16, 2007, a car bomb exploded near the Izdihar Compound in Baghdad, where a US diplomat was conferring with Iraqi officials. American security officials ordered a team ... to evacuate the diplomat to the Green Zone. Another Blackwater team, Raven 23, headed out of the Green Zone to block traffic at the Nisur Square traffic circle and thus assure the diplomat's safe passage back.... Raven 23 positioned its four vehicles on the south side of the Square and its members starting gesturing to stop traffic. Shots were fired; the dispute over who fired at whom and when is the substantive crux of the criminal case underlying this appeal. When the shooting stopped, 14 Iraqi citizens were dead and 20 wounded").

[46] Or those accompanying such individuals, H.R. 2136, §2(a)(3), proposed 18 USC. 3272(e)(1)(C), (2)(A)(ii); S. 1145, §2(a)(1)(C), proposed 18 USC. 3272(d)(1)(C), (2)(A)(ii).

[47] H.R. 2136, §7; S. 1145, §5(a)("Nothing in this Act or any amendment made by this Act shall be construed – (1) to limit or affect the application of extraterritorial jurisdiction related to any other Federal law").

[48] 18 USC. 6 ("As used in this title: The term 'department' means one of the executive departments enumerated in section 1 of Title 5, unless the context shows that such term was intended to describe the executive, legislative, or judicial branches of the government. The term 'agency' includes any department, independent establishment, commission, administration, authority, board or bureau of the United States or any corporation in which the United States has a proprietary interest, unless the context shows that such term was intended to be used in a more limited sense"); see also *Hubbard v. United States*, 514 US 695, 715 (1995)(overruling *United States v. Bramblett*, 348 US 503 (1955) which had held that the term agency or department of the United States in 18 USC. 1001 as then written included legislative branch entities).

[49] 18 USC. 3261(a).

[50] OMB, *Statement of Administration Policy: H.R. 2740 – MEJA Expansion and Enforcement Act of 2007* (Oct. 3, 2007), available at www. cq.com/graphics/hotdocs/27131-sapon-hr2740-10307.pdf.

[51] The list appears as attachment to this report.

[52] A second attachment lists the special maritime and territorial offenses.

[53] OM), *Statement of Administration Policy: H.R. 2740 – MEJA Expansion and Enforcement Act of 2007* (Oct. 3, 2007), available at www. cq.com/graphics/hotdocs/27131-sapon-hr2740-10307.pdf. *Holding Criminals Accountable: Extending Criminal Jurisdiction for Government Contractors and Employees Abroad: Hearing Before the Senate Comm. on the Judiciary*, 112th Cong., 1st sess. (2011)(statement of Ass't Att'y Gen. Lanny A. Breuer)("It is essential that any legislation include a statutory carve-out to ensure that the legislation does not impose criminal liability on authorized intelligence activities of the United States Government. The absence of an explicit exemption for authorized intelligence activities conducted abroad would negatively impact the United States' ability to conduct such activities").

[54] H.R. 2136, §2(a)(3), proposed 18 USC. 3272(d); S. 1145, §5(b).

[55] H.R. 2136, §7; S. 1145, §5(a); both citing 22 USC. 3927 with respect to authority and responsibility of a Chief of Mission.

[56] 18 USC. 3262. The Posse Comitatus Act, enacted after the Civil War, outlaws use of the Army or the Air Force to execute law unless expressly authorized by the Constitution or Act of Congress, 18 USC. 1385. "The Posse Comitatus Act ... is generally understood not to apply outside the United States.... In any event, however, the specific language of the Act [MEJA] empowering military law enforcement officials to make arrests should be seen as controlling over the nineteenth century statute's general prohibition," Schmitt, *Closing the Gap in Criminal Jurisdiction Over Civilians Accompanying the Armed Forces Abroad – A First Person Account of the Creation of the Military Extraterritorial Jurisdiction Act*, 51 CATHOLIC UNIVERSITY LAW REVIEW 55, 118 n.295 (2001).

[57] *Id.* at 118-19 & n.301 (footnote 301 in pertain part in brackets)("[T]he Military Extraterritorial Jurisdiction Act of 2000 contains an unusual and complex pair of sections. One section limits the power of the government to return a defendant to the United States until certain condition have been met and the other section requires some of the initial proceedings in a case to be held before the defendant is returned to the United States. These provisions were added to the bill during the House deliberations on House bill 3380 to address the concerns of the ACLU and FEA. [.... At the hearing n the bill, an FEA representative expressed concern that House bill 3380, as it was introduced, would have allowed the government to forcibly return a person to the United States soon after allegations against herm were lodged with authorities, but before any real investigation into the merits of the allegations had occurred.... FEA's main concern was that innocent defendants might have to bear the expensive costs of returning to a far away duty station once charges against them had been dismissed]").

[58] F.R.Crim.P. 5(a)(1)(B).

[59] 18 USC. 3265(a)(1).

[60] 18 USC. 3265(c), (a)(2), (a)(3).

[61] 18 USC. 3264.

[62] H.R. 2136, §2(a)(3), proposed 18 USC. 3273; S. 1145, §2(a)(1)(C), proposed 18 USC. 3273.

[63] H.R. 2136, §3(a)(B).

[64] OMB, *Statement of Administration Policy: H.R. 2740 – MEJA Expansion and Enforcement Act of 2007* (Oct. 3, 2007), available at www. cq.com/graphics/hotdocs/27131-sapon-hr2740-10307.pdf.

[65] H.R. 2136, §3(a), (b); S. 1145, §3(a), (b).

[66] H.R. 2136, §3(b)(4), (2); S. 1145, §3(b)(4), (2).

[67] H.R. 2136, §3(b)(5); S. 1145, §3(b)(5).

[68] See generally, CRS Report RL31253, *Statutes of Limitation in Federal Criminal Cases: An Overview*, by Charles Doyle.

[69] *Toussie v. United States*, 397 US 112, 115 (1970); *United States v. Palomino Garcia*, 606 F.3d 1317, 1323 (11th Cir. 2010); *United States v. Bucci*, 582 F.3d 108, 115 (1st Cir. 2009).

[70] *United States v. McMillan*, 600 F.3d 434, 444 (5th Cir. 2010)("An indictment charging a defendant with a federal non-capital crime generally must be returned within five years after commission of the offense. Once an indictment is filed, the limitations period is tolled on the charges set forth in the indictment"); United States v. Hickey, 580 F.3d 922, 929 (9th Cir. 2009); *United States v. Hoffecker*, 530 F.3d 137, 157 (3d Cir. 2008)("The statute of limitations requires that indictments for mail fraud and for conspiracy to commit mail and wire fraud must be found within five years of the commission of the offense. An indictment is found when it is returned by a grand jury and filed").

[71] *Toussie v. United States*, 397 US at 114-15.

[72] 18 USC. 3282.

[73] 18 USC. 3295.

[74] 18 USC. 3281, 3286(b), 3299, respectively. In rare cases, a want of timely prosecution may implicate a Sixth Amendment right to speedy trial, *Barker v. Wingo*, 407 US 514, 530-33 (1972), or a Fifth Amendment right to due process, *United States v. Lovasco*, 431 US 783, 788-89 (1977).

[75] 18 USC. 3287.

[76] 18 USC. 3290.

[77] H.R. 2136, §5(a), proposed 18 USC. 3302; S. 1145, §2(c), proposed 3287A.

[78] US Const. Amend. VI ("In all criminal prosecutions, the accused shall enjoy the right to a speedy and public trial, by an impartial jury of the State and district where the crime shall have been committed.... "); Art. III, §2, cl.3 ("The Trial of all Crimes ... shall be held in the State where the said Crimes shall have been committed; but when not committed within any State, the Trial shall be at such Place or Places as the Congress may by Law have directed"). See generally, CRS Report RL33223, *Venue: A Legal Analysis of Where a Federal Crime May Be Tried*, by Charles Doyle.

[79] 18 USC. 3238 ("The trial of all offenses begun or committed upon the high seas, or elsewhere out of the jurisdiction of any particular State or district, shall be in the district in which the offender, or any one of two or more joint offenders, is arrested or is first brought; but if such offender or offenders are not so arrested or brought into any district, an indictment or information may be filed in the district of the last known residence of the offender or of any one of two or more joint offenders, or if no such residence is known the indictment or information may be filed in the District of Columbia").

[80] 2 Wright & Henning, FEDERAL PRACTICE AND PROCEDURE: CRIMINAL §304 (4th ed. 2009).

[81] H.R. 2136, §4(a), proposed 18 USC. 3245; S. 1145, §2(b), proposed 18 USC. 3245 ("In addition to any venue otherwise provided in this chapter, the trial of any offense involving a violation of section 3261, 3271, or 3272 of this title may be brought – (1) in the district in which is headquartered the department or agency of the United States that employs the offender, or any one of two or more joint offenders, or (2) in the district in which is headquartered the department or agency of the United States that the offender is accompanying, or that any one of two or more joint offenders is accompanying"); language in italics appears only in the Senate bill.

[82] Id.

[83] S. 1145, §2(b), proposed 18 USC. 3245.

[84] 18 USC. 3142(g)("The judicial officer shall, in determining whether there are conditions of release that will reasonably assure the appearance of the person as required ... take into account ... the characteristics of the person including ... the person's ... employment, financial resources, length of residence in the community, community ties...."). A person tried in a district remote from his home has no length of residence in the community where the trial is to be held; is not likely to have community ties there; and may have difficulty continuing his employment while preparing for trial in a remote location.

In: Extraterritorial Application ...
Editors: D. Garcia and G. Coleman ISBN 978-1-62081-445-1

Chapter 3

STATEMENT OF SENATOR PATRICK LEAHY (D-VT.), CHAIRMAN, SENATE JUDICIARY COMMITTEE, HEARING ON "HOLDING CRIMINALS ACCOUNTABLE: EXTENDING CRIMINAL JURISDICTION TO GOVERNMENT CONTRACTORS AND EMPLOYEES ABROAD"*

May 25, 2011

Today, the Committee considers the need to ensure accountability for crimes committed by Government contractors and employees abroad. President Obama has been working hard to improve America's credibility in the world, our reputation for justice, and our commitment to the rule of law. A key component of that important mission is ensuring accountability for those who represent us overseas.

Accountability is crucial, not just for our image abroad and our diplomatic relations, but for ensuring our national security.

To promote accountability, Congress must make sure that our criminal laws reach serious misconduct by American Government employees and contractors wherever they act. That is why I introduced the Civilian

* This is an edited, reformatted and augmented version of statement given on May 25, 2011. before the Committee on the Judiciary United States Senate.

Extraterritorial Jurisdiction Act in the last Congress, and I will soon introduce similar legislation this year.

Tragic events in Iraq in 2007 made clear the need to strengthen the laws providing for jurisdiction over American Government employees and contractors working abroad. In September 2007, Blackwater security contractors working for the State Department shot more than 20 unarmed civilians on the streets of Baghdad, killing at least 14 of them, and causing a rift in our relations with the Iraqi government.

Efforts to prosecute those responsible for these shootings have been fraught with difficulties, and our ability to hold the wrongdoers in this case accountable remains in doubt. Had jurisdiction for these offenses been clear, FBI agents likely would have been on the scene immediately, which could well have prevented the problems that have plagued the case.

Other incidents have made all too clear that the Blackwater case was not an isolated incident. Private security contractors have been involved in violent incidents and serious misconduct in Iraq and Afghanistan, including other shooting incidents in which civilians have been seriously injured or killed. In these cases too, there have not been prosecutions.

In the last Congress, the Senate Judiciary Committee heard testimony from Jamie Leigh Jones, a young woman from Texas who took a job with Halliburton in Iraq in 2005 when she was 20-years-old. In her first week on the job, she was drugged and gang-raped by co-workers. When she reported this assault, her employers moved her to a locked trailer, where she was kept by armed guards and freed only when the State Department intervened.

Ms. Jones testified about the arbitration clause in her contract that prevented her from suing Halliburton for this outrageous conduct, and Congress has moved to change the civil law to prevent that kind of injustice. Criminal jurisdiction over these kinds of atrocious crimes abroad, however, remains complicated, depending too greatly on the specific location of the crime, making prosecutions inconsistent and sometimes impossible. We must fix the law to help avoid arbitrary injustice and ensure that victims will not see their attackers escape accountability.

I worked with Senator Sessions and others in 2000 to pass the Military Extraterritorial Jurisdiction Act, and then again to amend it in 2004, so that US criminal laws would extend to all members of the US military, to those who accompany them, and to contractors who work with the military.

The next step is to establish clearly that all US government employees and contractors who commit crimes while working abroad - whether they work with the military or not - can be charged and tried in the United States. As the military withdraws from Iraq and Afghanistan, the American presence in those countries will consist largely of civilian employees and contractors. There must be accountability for all of those who represent our Government overseas. And in those instances where the local justice system may be less fair, this explicit jurisdiction will also protect Americans by providing the option of prosecuting them in the United States, rather than leaving them subject to hostile and unpredictable local courts.

Ensuring criminal accountability will also improve our national security. Our allies, including those countries most essential to our counter-terrorism and national security efforts, work best with us when we hold our own accountable. We cannot afford the distrust created by employees and contractors acting with impunity and disregard for the rule of law, as so clearly happened in the Blackwater case. Moreover, the talented men and women we need to advance our national security efforts will be more likely to step forward and serve if we stamp out the lawless atmosphere in places like Iraq and Afghanistan. That is why the Civilian Extraterritorial Jurisdiction Act is supported by people like Ignacio Balderas, CEO of security contractor Triple Canopy.

In the past, legislation in this area has been bipartisan. I hope it will be again. I have been working with the Justice Department to make this legislation better and particularly to ensure that the legislation will be formulated in a way that will ensure criminal accountability, but will not impact the conduct of US intelligence agencies abroad. I hope that we will be able to rapidly pass this important reform into law with bipartisan support. I look forward to hearing from our witnesses about how we can move forward on this important issue.

In: Extraterritorial Application ...
Editors: D. Garcia and G. Coleman ISBN 978-1-62081-445-1

Chapter 4

STATEMENT OF TARA LEE, GLOBAL CO-CHAIR, TRANSNATIONAL LITIGATION DLA PIPER LLP (US). HEARING ON "HOLDING CRIMINALS ACCOUNTABLE: EXTENDING CRIMINAL JURISDICTION TO GOVERNMENT CONTRACTORS AND EMPLOYEES ABROAD"*

May 25, 2011

Mr. Chairman, Senator Grassley, and other distinguished members of the Committee, thank you for the opportunity to appear before you today. I know that each of you share the deep respect and appreciation that I feel for the men and women of the defense contracting community, especially for those individuals who endure arduous conditions and unstable environments so that they can serve alongside and support the armed forces. I want to thank you for the opportunity to address you today and to thank you for the work you have undertaken on behalf of veterans, military members and their families, and contractors. As someone who has served in the Navy, been the spouse of an Army soldier, and is now a member of the contracting community, I want to thank you on behalf of each of those communities for what you do for us.

---

* This is an edited, reformatted and augmented version of statement given on May 25, 2011. before the Committee on the Judiciary United States Senate.

The issue today – extraterritorial jurisdiction and accountability for contractors – does not engender a great deal of controversy or dissent. It is not, and should not be, a partisan matter. Nether is it an issue where the US judicial system and the contracting community are at odds. We all share a commitment to serving the national security objectives of the United States of America. I think we also share a desire for there to be clarity in the accountability mechanisms that reach our citizens. When the accountability mechanism is focused on those individuals who serve in harm's way on our behalf, whether they be uniformed or not, the obligation to provide them with clarity is especially strong.

I am a Naval Academy graduate, a former military lawyer, and a former fellow at the Center for the Study of Professional Military Ethics at the US Naval Academy, where I studied and taught battlefield accountability. In my current practice I both advise companies on mitigating their risks and training their employees to operate in conflict environments, and represent companies when they face government investigations and civil or criminal litigation. I have also devoted several thousand hours of pro bono legal work to the representation of victims of the horrific war crimes that occurred in Somalia in the 1980's, victims who, because no jurisdiction had the capacity or will to take criminal action, had no hope of achieving redress other than through the civil courts of the United States. These experiences each contribute to my very broad perspective on the importance of clarity in criminal accountability mechanisms.

From my experience – and I speak today from the perspective of an attorney who currently manages a law practice group specializing in representing government contractors – the Military Extraterritorial Jurisdiction Act standing alone has not provided that clarity. As you know, the Act has been subject to legal challenge as to the breadth of its jurisdiction, as it applies on its face only to those contractors who are "employed by or accompanying the Armed Forces outside the United States." Arguably, MEJA by its plain text does not apply to those contractors working for the State Department or for government agencies other than the Department of Defense.

Clarity and certainty is as important to the contracting community as it is to the government. Companies have an obligation to their employees to properly advise them of the legal rights, risks, and accountability mechanisms to which they are subject when serving overseas. A continued absence of clarity on whether MEJA applies to civilian employees working on nonDoD contracts does not serve the interests of the contracting community or its employees. For example, a company with both Department of Defense and

Department of State contracts might, under the current statutory framework, accurately advise employees working on its Defense contracts that they "are" subject to MEJA jurisdiction, while advising employees doing similar work in the same location but on a State Department contract that they "might be" subject to MEJA jurisdiction. Neither the statute itself nor the limited number of available judicial interpretations make the effective reach of MEJA completely clear. Thus the Civilian Extraterritorial Jurisdiction Act has the potential to provide more certainty regarding the application of US criminal law to overseas contractors.

Not only would CEJA provide more jurisdictional certainty, it would also enable the prompt and professional investigation of potentially criminal incidents. Civilian companies, especially those operating under the often arduous conditions of contingency operations, are neither empowered to perform nor well-suited to perform the sovereign functions of law enforcement and criminal investigation. Moreover, contractors often operate in unstable environments where the host nation capacities for criminal justice functions are limited or developing. Companies operating in those environments are much better served if adequate US government resources are available to assist with or to provide the function. CEJA also provides the personnel and resources to address that need.

I know you have received written statements of support from several companies directly and from the International Stability Operations Association, a trade organization representing stability operations contractors, as well as from organizations in the human rights community. The Commission for Wartime Contracting also recently called for clarification in criminal jurisdiction over civilian-agency contractors. This diverse recognition of the need for an appropriately crafted CEJA reflects, I think, the universal recognition that accountability for criminal wrongdoers is a critical component of securing our nation's foreign policy goals. No-one wants to operate in an environment of uncertain legal clarity, least of all companies who are already operating in often unstable environments.

Thank you again for the opportunity to discuss this important topic with you today and I look forward to answering any questions you might have.

In: Extraterritorial Application ...
Editors: D. Garcia and G. Coleman

ISBN 978-1-62081-445-1

Chapter 5

STATEMENT BY GEOFFREY S. CORN, PROFESSOR OF LAW, SOUTH TEXAS COLLEGE OF LAW, HOUSTON, TEXAS; LIEUTENANT COLONEL, US ARMY (RETIRED)*

I would first like to thank the Committee for providing me the opportunity to share my perspective on the importance of enacting the Civilian Extraterritorial Jurisdiction Act (CEJA).

As a soldier and military staff officer I was taught to express my "bottom-line up front," and my bottom-line is that Congress should enact this statute. Indeed, I believe the expansion of federal civilian jurisdiction over contractors associated with the US government is not only consistent with the national security interests of the nation, but is also clearly in the best interest of the US armed forces. From a national security perspective, CEJA will contribute to the deterrence of contractor misconduct by placing contractors on clear notice that such misconduct is subject to federal criminal sanction, and will reduce the risk that the credibility of US operations will be compromised by a perception of impunity for contractor misconduct. From a military perspective, CEJA will reduce the possibility that the military will be called upon to assert jurisdiction over contractors because of a lack of viable alternatives to address contractor misconduct.

* This is an edited, reformatted and augmented version of statement given on May 25, 2011. before the Committee on the Judiciary United States Senate.

Civilians – both civil servants and contractors – are unquestionably essential to executing the broad range of missions related to achieving the national security objective of the nation. While it is not a new phenomenon to rely on civilians to support external efforts to achieve these objectives, the numbers of civilians and range of missions performed is unprecedented in our history. Indeed, the changing nature of the strategic framework associated with executing our national security strategy will continue to push civilians into a range of functions not seen previously. In the era of conventional military threats, we rightly anticipated that employment of civilians abroad would be predominately associated with the armed forces. Unlike prior eras, the increasing imperative of inter-agency participation in the execution of national security strategy has resulted in robust presence of civilians operating in support of both the Department of Defense and other federal agencies.

This trend, coupled with the post-cold war emphasis on increasing the "tooth to tail" ratio of military deployments, has produced the inevitable reality of civilian misconduct in relation to these missions. Prior to 1970, trial by courts-martial served as the primary mechanism for responding to such misconduct. This was the result of two influences. First, civilians supporting US national security objectives normally operated in association with the armed forces. Second, the exercise of military jurisdiction over such civilians was considered consistent with both the tradition of military law and the Constitution. This latter influence was fundamentally undermined when the Court of Military Appeals (the predecessor to the Court of Appeals for the Armed Forces) decided the case of *United States v. Averette* (19 C.M.A. 363, 41 C.M.R. 363 (1970)). That decision held that the jurisdiction over civilians accompanying the armed forces established by Congress in the Uniform Code of Military Justice (UCMJ) applied only during periods of formally declared war. As a result of this opinion (and the assumption that a formally declared war was a highly unlikely event), an entire generation of Judge Advocates learned that it was almost inconceivable that civilians would ever again be subject to military jurisdiction.

The impunity for civilian misconduct created by this jurisdictional void became apparent as the US military focused increasingly on expeditionary operations in the decade following the end of the Cold War. In response, Congress sought to fill the void by enacting the Military Extraterritorial Jurisdiction Act (MEJA). This law reflected a clear preference for Article III civilian trial for civilians who commit misconduct when operating in association with the armed forces outside the United States, a preference perceived as logical by the military. However, a perception of contractor impunity arose during the decade following MEJA's enactment as the result of jurisdictional and implementation limitations of the statute, with certain high profile cases of civilian contractor misconduct in Iraq and Afghanistan drawing particular attention. In an apparent response to this perception, in 2006 Congress amended the UCMJ to resurrect military jurisdiction over civilians accompanying the armed forces in the field. By explicitly including contingency operations within the scope of that jurisdiction, Congress overrode Averette's "formally declared war" limitation.

This resurrection took military legal experts by surprise. Having come of age in the post Averette era, many of these experts assumed that the Constitution barred asserting military jurisdiction over civilians beyond the limited context of war crimes. This assumption was informed by both Averette and *Reid v. Covert* (354 US 1 (1957)) – a seminal Supreme Court decision related to the application of Bill of Rights protections to US citizens outside the United States. Ried's core holding was that trying spouses of US service-members stationed abroad by courts-martial (even when authorized by international agreement) for capital offenses deprived these citizens of the protections of the Fifth and Sixth Amendment. However, Ried struck down the assertion of military jurisdiction over US civilians only in locations with a mature presence of US forces (like the United Kingdom, Japan, Germany, and other NATO allied nations); it did not address the assertion of such jurisdiction over civilians accompanying the armed forces in the field. In fact, the Court specifically excluded such jurisdiction from its decision.

While Averette relied heavily on Reid, it is clear that the resurrection of military jurisdiction over civilians accompanying the armed forces during contingency operations was not clearly unconstitutional. Nonetheless, as I have written in the attached law review article, this resurrection does raise significant constitutional questions. If the exercise of military jurisdiction over civilians is understood as a measure of last resort – as I believe it must be based on our historic aversion to the intrusion of military authority into the realm of civil affairs – then the enactment of federal criminal statutes like MEJA and the War Crimes Act (and the overall increases in long-arm federal criminal jurisdiction) represents a fundamental change in circumstances from the pre-Averette era. Prior to this evolution of federal criminal law, military jurisdiction provided near exclusive criminal jurisdiction over civilians accompanying the armed forces in the field. It is therefore unsurprising that since the inception of the nation, military courts have been vested with such jurisdiction. Today, however, this is no longer the case. As a result, the imprimatur of necessity no longer provides a compelling justification for subjecting civilians to military criminal jurisdiction.

This is not to suggest that I consider courts-martial somehow defective. Indeed, it is my belief that trial by court-martial is fundamentally fair, and in many respects more protective of an accused's right to a fair trial than Article III trials. However, courts-martial process simply does not afford the full panoply of rights to a criminal defendant provided by the Constitution. Most notably, trial by courts-martial does not require Grand Jury indictment, life tenured judges, or a jury composed of the defendant's peers. While these differences have historically been considered acceptable for members of the armed forces subject to the special criminal justice system of the military, it is difficult to justify subjecting civilians to criminal trials absent these protections unless doing so is a genuine measure of last resort. In my opinion, most civilians would simply not understand why a civilian would be tried in such a unique criminal system, being judged not by a jury of his or her peers but instead by a panel of military officers.

It is because of this I believe it was critically important to enact MEJA. However, MEJA was based on an assumption that has become increasingly stale: that civilians present in areas of military operations will be connected to the military by employment or contract. Civilians supporting the complex missions of today, although often operating in close proximity with the military, are routinely connected to other government agencies. The employment or contractual relationship between these civilians and the US government places them outside the scope of MEJA jurisdiction, producing the same type of jurisdictional gap MEJA sought to close. CEJA is therefore a necessary complement to MEJA. Its enactment will ensure all civilians present in operational areas as the result of an employment or contractual relationship with the United States (other than host nation nationals) are subject to federal civilian criminal jurisdiction. As a result, it will reduce the likelihood that the military will be called upon to exercise criminal jurisdiction over incidents of misconduct committed by these civilians, thereby averting the complex policy and constitutional issues resulting trying civilians by courts-martial.

I also support the enumeration of offenses in CEJA. While MEJA employs the alternate method of incorporating Title 18 offenses, I believe the enumeration approach provides two important benefits. First, it provides clear notice of the scope of criminal proscription imposed on civilians subject to CEJA. Second, it limits the type of offenses that might result in a CEJA prosecution to serious crimes. This latter benefit also reveals another concern with subjecting civilians to UCMJ jurisdiction. When Congress amended the

UCMJ to resurrect military jurisdiction over civilians accompanying the force, it in no way limited the offenses applicable to civilians. As a result, that amendment subjects civilians to every offense in the military code – a range of offenses that extends beyond serious common law crimes and includes unique military offenses. While I believe it is unlikely that a military commander would pursue charges against a civilian for unique military offenses (such as disobedience of orders, absence without official leave, or dereliction of duty), CEJA would substantially reduce even the risk of such an odd assertion of military jurisdiction.

There are other situations where CEJA, like MEJA, could prove quite beneficial, most notably for addressing acts of misconduct by civilian employees and family members serving abroad in more stable environments. Military experience over the decades indicates that there are times when these civilians engage in misconduct that the host nation is either not interested in, or does not have valid jurisdiction to address. CEJA would provide a means for prosecuting acts of serious misconduct committed by civilians associated with US government agencies in other countries. In fact, the ability to exercise such jurisdiction might result in the host nation foregoing prosecution at the request of the US government even when they initially pursue such cases, allowing the US civilian to be prosecuted in the United States instead of a foreign jurisdiction.

Ultimately, I can see no good reason not to enact CEJA. While I don't think it is possible to guarantee that resort to military jurisdiction for civilian misconduct will never be necessary and appropriate, I believe enhancing the scope of federal civilian jurisdiction over civilians abroad is an important means of limiting such resort to situations of genuine necessity. MEJA was the first step in achieving that goal; CEJA will be the next. The ever increasing reliance on civilian support to US government functions abroad necessitates an ability to ensure accountability for the small minority of civilians who engage in misconduct. Unless federal civilian criminal jurisdiction is comprehensive, pressure to resort to the broad grant of military jurisdiction over civilians resurrected by the 2006 amendment to the UCMJ is almost inevitable. It is therefore in the interests of the nation, the military, and potential civilian defendants to enact CEJA.

In: Extraterritorial Application ... ISBN 978-1-62081-445-1
Editors: D. Garcia and G. Coleman

Chapter 6

STATEMENT OF MICHAEL J. EDNEY GIBSON, DUNN & CRUTCHER LLP. HEARING ON "HOLDING CRIMINALS ACCOUNTABLE: EXTENDING CRIMINAL JURISDICTION TO GOVERNMENT CONTRACTORS AND EMPLOYEES ABROAD"*

May 25, 2011

Chairman Leahy, Ranking Member Grassley, and distinguished members of the Committee, thank you for giving me the opportunity to testify on this important subject.[1] The United States is conducting military operations in two foreign theaters of combat and maintains diplomatic outposts throughout the world. Holding accountable representatives of the United States—whether its employees or its contractors—who engage in serious misconduct abroad is thus a recurring and complex matter. Current federal law arguably does not provide authority to prosecute some notable incidents of potential misconduct overseas by contractors or employees unassociated with the Department of Defense. The Congress and the Executive Branch have struggled with the appropriate legislative approach to this dilemma through at least two Administrations.

---

* This is an edited, reformatted and augmented version of statement given on May 25, 2011. before the Committee on the Judiciary United States Senate.

Addressing this problem, however, requires exceptional caution and attention to detail to protect ongoing and future intelligence and other national security operations. Legislation that extends outside the United States a wide range of federal criminal laws to employees and contractors *of all federal government agencies*, including our intelligence agencies, without careful review and appropriate exceptions, would present a particular risk to national security.

I. CURRENT LAW AND FOREIGN POLICY CHALLENGES

Current law provides mechanisms for punishing misconduct by certain U.S. government employees and contractors that occurs outside the United States. The Uniform Code of Military Justice ("UCMJ") establishes prohibitions and obligations that apply outside the United States,[2] the violation of which can result in sanctions similar to the criminal justice system.[3] These regulations were crafted with the realities of foreign armed conflict in mind. The UCMJ applies not only to members of the active and reserve units of our armed forces, but also to persons (such as contractors and civilian employees) who serve with or accompany our armed forces overseas.[4]

In 2000, the Congress passed and the President signed the Military Extraterritorial Jurisdiction Act ("MEJA").[5] That Act, as amended in 2004, applies a discrete set of federal criminal felonies overseas to members of the military and certain individuals who support or accompany the armed forces.[6] Conducting military operations under multiple and newly applicable federal criminal prohibitions ordinarily would present challenges. But MEJA sought to avoid these difficulties by ensuring the primacy, in most circumstances, of the UCMJ and its long history of regulating the conduct of armed conflicts.[7]

These two laws, however, stop short of U.S. government employees and contractors not closely associated with the Department of Defense. For example, our diplomats abroad or the security personnel who support the Department of State would not automatically fall under MEJA or the UCMJ.[8]

This condition can raise foreign policy challenges, particularly in foreign countries where U.S. troops are deployed for combat operations. Those operations are often conducted under a status of forces agreement concluded with the governments of those countries, should a recognized government exist. In those agreements, the United States customarily seeks immunity for all of its employees and contractors—whether associated with the military or not— from the criminal procedures of the foreign state. This immunity is important, as the nature of combat operations can inflame passions that may lead to foreign government prosecutions unwarranted by the evidence. One argument the United States makes in negotiations for this immunity is the existence of mechanisms for the United States to address the misconduct of our own troops, employees, and contractors. This argument can be unpersuasive, however, when relevant law does not reach certain notable groups of U.S. government employees and contractors in the theater. The United States faced this challenge in negotiating the 2008 status of forces agreement with the Government of Iraq and ultimately accepted a narrowed immunity for its employees and contractors from the Iraqi criminal justice system.[9]

II. Previous Efforts to Extend Federal Criminal Law Overseas to U.S. Government Employees and Contractors Unassociated with the Department of Defense

Several Congressmen and Senators introduced versions of legislation in the 110th Congress seeking to apply certain federal criminal laws overseas to a wider set of U.S. government employees and contractors. A form of such legislation advanced furthest in the House of Representatives—H.R. 2740, entitled the "MEJA Expansion and Enforcement Act."[10] That bill sought to expand MEJA to employees and contractors *of any U.S. government agency* acting in an area, such as Iraq or Afghanistan, where the U.S. military is "conducting a contingency operation."[11] The bill tracked MEJA in the substantive scope of applicable offenses, seeking to criminalize conduct that would have been a federal felony "if the conduct had been engaged in within the special maritime and territorial jurisdiction of the United States."[12]

The Administration of President George W. Bush raised serious concerns about this bill. A Statement of Administration Policy issued on October 3, 2007, explained that "[t]he bill would have unintended and intolerable consequences for crucial and necessary national security activities and operations."[13] Recognizing this dilemma, the version of H.R. 2740 ultimately passed by the House of Representatives included an attempt to carve from its coverage intelligence operations.[14] The Administration and Senate staff subsequently discussed potential text for a carve-out or exception to protect national security and intelligence operations. Never reaching agreement, the

110th Congress adjourned without presenting to the President legislation on this subject.

III. UNLESS CAREFULLY DRAFTED, EXPANDING FEDERAL CRIMINAL LAW TO THE EMPLOYEES AND CONTRACTORS OF ALL U.S. GOVERNMENT AGENCIES WILL THREATEN IMPORTANT NATIONAL SECURITY AND INTELLIGENCE OPERATIONS

Any legislative measure to expand federal criminal law abroad to all government employees and contractors must carefully address the effect on national security operations.

I have reviewed S. 2979, entitled the "Civilian Extraterritorial Jurisdiction Act of 2010." It contains many of the same concerning features as H.R. 2740 introduced in the 110th Congress. Certainly, S. 2979 would authorize the prosecution of future misconduct by, for example, private security contractors protecting State Department diplomats in Iraq. At the same time, however, S. 2979 would apply wide swaths of federal criminal law to employees and contractors of our intelligence agencies and would revolutionize the carefully drawn set of legal restrictions that governs the activities of those agencies. This was the same problem presented by early drafts of H.R. 2740 in the 110th Congress. Importantly, S. 2979 lacks an exception for or any method of protecting crucial intelligence and national security operations from prosecution.[15] Three points are important here.

First, in part because of the effect on overseas national security or intelligence operations, the Congress has been careful explicitly to apply only a very limited set of criminal offenses to conduct occurring wholly outside the territory of the United States. The limited set of offenses with relevant extraterritorial effect include the anti-torture statute,[16] the War Crimes Act,[17] certain anti-human trafficking statutes,[18] the treason statute,[19] and the anti-genocide statute.[20]

The Congress should continue its practice of giving wholly extraterritorial effect to criminal statutes only after careful and informed study of their effects on national security and intelligence operations. Most notably in this regard, legislation proposed to cover all U.S. government employees and contractors, including those of our intelligence agencies, has tended to incorporate laws enacted to govern the Special Maritime and Territorial Jurisdiction of the

United States ("SMTJ").[21] The SMTJ includes areas where the federal Government would perform the functions of a primary sovereign, without the assistance of a State government, such as foreign military bases and embassies or aboard U.S. registered vessels. Federal criminal offenses for the SMTJ supply the type of public order crimes that residents of a city in the United States would expect their State and local governments to enact, including prohibitions on burglary, robbery, manslaughter, and assault.[22]

The inclusion of SMTJ offenses is particularly significant given the novelty of their application to intelligence operations. The current law of the Military Extraterritorial

Jurisdiction Act, at first glance, also applies SMTJ offenses to members of the military while outside the United States.[23] But MEJA protects our armed forces when conducting military operations abroad by not displacing or supplementing the UCMJ, with limited exceptions.[24] The UCMJ has a long tradition of responsibly governing what can be violent military activities, and our armed forces can take comfort that the UCMJ ordinarily will not punish them for doing their jobs. Also when applied in areas of exclusive federal jurisdiction, SMTJ crimes as customary public order offenses draw on extensive bodies of law protecting activities similar to those of domestic law enforcement. But there is no such custom protecting intelligence activities abroad from general public order offenses, because they have never applied outside the United States.

Legislation extending SMTJ offenses to all government employees throughout the world thus places intelligence activities at particular risk.

It is difficult to address in an open hearing how these offenses, if applicable to all federal government employees and contractors while outside the United States, might affect intelligence or other national security operations. For purposes of this setting, I strongly agree with Assistant Attorney General Breuer that the Congress should explicitly except national security and intelligence activities from the contemplated expansion of criminal law abroad. Legislation with an appropriately strong exception would prevent interference with vital national security and intelligence operations, while authorizing future prosecutions, if appropriate, in circumstances similar to recent difficult cases. Alleged grave misconduct by diplomatic security personnel, and civilian employees and contractors' outrageous and embarrassing offenses against the civilians of foreign countries, often committed on personal time while stationed abroad, come to mind. Any restrictions on intelligence activities should not be a byproduct of addressing an unrelated problem.

At a minimum, any legislative effort in this area that lacks a broad national security exception must not proceed without a fully informed evaluation of how various criminal laws, never before applied abroad, would affect current and potential national security and intelligence operations. In such circumstances, committees of the Congress should hold closed hearings where they can address these issues with the benefit of classified information. The congressional intelligence committees, given their regular responsibility in setting rules for the conduct of intelligence operations and overseeing their execution, should have an important role in any such inquiry.

Second, the prospect of prosecutorial discretion would not solve the national security threat identified above. Some might say that the Department of Justice would not prosecute intelligence officers for carrying out authorized overseas operations, even if those officers transgressed one of the criminal statutes the proposed legislation would make applicable. In my experience, however, intelligence officers and their supervisors are generally unwilling to undertake an operation if a U.S. criminal statute potentially prohibits it. Nor should they be expected to rely for their continued liberty on the exercise of prosecutorial discretion after the fact. Without protection in statute, broad expansions of criminal laws abroad, leaving unanswered questions, may chill vital national security and intelligence activities.

Third, if legislation were to apply a wide selection of criminal offenses to intelligence and other national security activities, we should expect further strain on the Classified Information Procedures Act ("CIPA").[25] Several members of this Committee have noted the need for CIPA reform.[26] CIPA was enacted in 1980 to combat the threat of graymail in espionage prosecutions.[27] To that end, CIPA established elaborate, information-forcing procedures that require defendants to give notice before disclosing any classified information in open court.[28] As this Committee made clear when considering CIPA, the principal purpose of these procedures was to make manageable cases against U.S. government employees who possess classified information independently of anything that occurs in the criminal prosecution.[29]

Enforcement of a broad new set of criminal statutes against intelligence or national security operations abroad would be another application beyond the specific circumstance that prompted CIPA in 1980. The expansion of federal criminal law contemplated by the proposed legislation cannot be considered in isolation from efforts to update CIPA for the last three decades of new challenges.

* * *

Thank you again for the opportunity to discuss this important issue with the Committee. I am prepared to answer the Committee's questions.

End Notes

[1] The views expressed herein are my own and do not reflect those of Gibson, Dunn & Crutcher LLP.

[2] 10 U.S.C. §§ 805, 877–934.

[3] 10 U.S.C. §§ 855–858b.

[4] 10 U.S.C. § 802(a).

[5] Pub. L. No. 106-523, 114 Stat. 2488 (2000) (codified at 18 U.S.C. §§ 3261 *et seq.*).

[6] 18 U.S.C. § 3261(a).

[7] 18 U.S.C. § 3261(d).

[8] *See* 18 U.S.C. §§ 3261(a), 3267(1)–(2); 10 U.S.C. § 802(a).

[9] *Compare* Coalition Provisional Authority Order Number 17 (June 27, 2004), *with* Agreement Between the United States of America and the Republic of Iraq on Withdrawal of United States Forces from Iraq and the Organization of Their Activities During Their Temporary Presence in Iraq (Nov. 17, 2008).

[10] H.R. 2740, 110th Cong. (2007) (as introduced in House, June 15, 2007).

[11] *Id.* § 2(a)(1).

[12] 18 U.S.C. § 3261(a); *see* H.R. 2740, *supra* note 10, § 2(a)(1).

[13] Statement of Administration Policy: H.R. 2740—MEJA Expansion and Enforcement Act of 2007, American Presidency Project (Oct. 3, 2007), *available at* http://www.presidency.ucsb.edu/ws/index.php?pid=75852#ixzz1NBl5xagQ (last visited on May 24, 2011).

[14] H.R. 2740, 110th Cong. § 6 (2007) (as passed by House, Oct. 4, 2007).

[15] In addition, the geographic scope of the threat to intelligence operations presented by S. 2979 is broader because it would apply *worldwide*. H.R. 2740, by contrast, would have applied only in and around areas of a U.S. military contingency operation, such as Iraq and Afghanistan.

[16] 18 U.S.C. § 2340A.

[17] 18 U.S.C. § 2441.

[18] 18 U.S.C. §§ 3271-72.

[19] 18 U.S.C. § 2381.

[20] 18 U.S.C. § 1091.

[21] 18 U.S.C. § 7.

[22] 18 U.S.C. §§ 2111, 1112, 113.

[23] 18 U.S.C. § 3261(a).

[24] 18 U.S.C. § 3261(d).

[25] 18 U.S.C. app. 3 §§ 1–16.

[26] *See, e.g.*, Classified Information Procedures Reform Act, S. 1726, 111th Cong. §§ 201-05 (2009) (introduced by Sens. Kyl and Cornyn, Sept. 29, 2009).

[27] S. Rep. No. 96-456, *Classified Information Procedures Act* (June 18, 1980), *reprinted in* 1980 U.S.C.C.A.N. 4294, 4295.

[28] 18 U.S.C. §§ 2, 5–9.

[29] The Judiciary Committee's report of the bill explained the extensive study of "cases in which intelligence information had been passed to foreign powers through espionage or through leaks in the media." S. Rep. No. 96-456, *supra*, at 4295. The key finding of the Committee's study was that "prosecution of a defendant for disclosing national security information often requires the disclosure in the course of trial of the very information that the law seeks to protect." *Id.*

In: Extraterritorial Application …
Editors: D. Garcia and G. Coleman
ISBN 978-1-62081-445-1

Chapter 7

STATEMENT OF LANNY A. BREUER, ASSISTANT ATTORNEY GENERAL, CRIMINAL DIVISION DEPARTMENT OF JUSTICE. HEARING ON "HOLDING CRIMINALS ACCOUNTABLE: EXTENDING CRIMINAL JURISDICTION FOR GOVERNMENT CONTRACTORS AND EMPLOYEES ABROAD"*

May 25, 2011

I. INTRODUCTION

Chairman Leahy, Ranking Member Grassley, and distinguished Members of the Committee: Thank you for inviting me to speak with you today about the proposed Civilian Extraterritorial Jurisdiction Act, or CEJA.

I am honored to appear before you on behalf of the Department of Justice, where I am privileged to lead the Criminal Division's nearly 600 lawyers in enforcing the Federal criminal laws. Together with the Nation's 94 U.S. Attorneys' Offices, the Criminal Division's Human Rights and Special

* This is an edited, reformatted and augmented version of statement given on May 25, 2011. before the Committee on the Judiciary United States Senate.

Prosecutions Section investigates and prosecutes individuals under the existing Military Extraterritorial Jurisdiction Act, or MEJA, for crimes those individuals commit overseas. We have had great success in bringing cases under MEJA, and are committed to continuing to enforce MEJA vigorously.

As much as we have been able to accomplish under existing law, however, MEJA leaves significant gaps in our enforcement capability. In particular, under MEJA, certain civilian U.S. Government employees can commit crimes abroad, yet not be subject to the jurisdiction of U.S. courts. For example, a civilian Government contractor whose employment is unrelated to the mission of the Department of Defense – but is related to the mission of another U.S. Government agency – cannot currently be prosecuted under MEJA, even if he or she clearly committed a crime. CEJA would address this significant shortcoming by extending U.S. jurisdiction to all non-Department of Defense employees and contractors who commit crimes overseas.

II. BACKGROUND

The Military Extraterritorial Jurisdiction Act, 18 U.S.C. § 3261, *et seq.*, is the principal Federal statute used to prosecute certain U.S. Government employees, contractors, and their dependents who commit crimes overseas. As originally enacted, in 2000, MEJA applied only to certain narrow classes of individuals associated with the Department of Defense. In 2004, however, Congress amended MEJA, expanding it to cover civilian employees and contractors (and their dependents) of agencies other than the Department of Defense, but only to the extent that the employee's or contractor's employment "relates to supporting the mission of the Department of Defense overseas."

Since MEJA was enacted, the Justice Department has successfully prosecuted numerous MEJA cases involving former Department of Defense employees or individuals accompanying them overseas. In *United States v. Steven Green*, for example, the Justice Department secured a conviction in Louisville, Kentucky against a former Army soldier for the brutal rape and killing of a 14-year old Iraqi girl and the murders of three of her family members while the soldier was on active duty in Iraq. In *United States v. Rico Williams*, the Justice Department obtained a conviction in the District of Columbia against a former Air Force senior airman for a gang-initiation beating that ended in the death of an Army Sergeant in Germany. And in *United Statesv. Dwain Williams*, we obtained a jury conviction in Valdosta,

Georgia against an individual accompanying a military service member overseas for the aggravated sexual abuse of a child in Japan.

The Justice Department has also successfully prosecuted Defense Department contractors employed overseas. In *United States v. Christopher Drotleff, et al.*, for example, we obtained jury convictions in Norfolk, Virginia of two Department of Defense contractors for involuntary manslaughter of a civilian in Afghanistan. In *United States v. Sean T. Brehm*, we secured a conviction from a Department of Defense contractor on charges of assault with a deadly weapon in Afghanistan. And in *United States v. Jorge Thornton*, we secured a conviction from a Department of Defense contractor for abusive sexual contact while working at a U.S. military Forward Operating Base in Iraq. We have also investigated and prosecuted non-Department of Defense contractors whose work related to "supporting the mission of the Department of Defense overseas."

The Justice Department also successfully and aggressively uses every other tool now available to us to prosecute crimes committed abroad by U.S. Government personnel and U.S. Government contractors (which can include both U.S. citizens and citizens of other countries). We can and do prosecute crimes committed within the special maritime and territorial jurisdiction (SMTJ) of the United States. In *United States v. Andrew Warren*, for example, a former official with the Central Intelligence Agency (CIA) was sentenced in the District of Columbia to 65 months in prison for abusive sexual contact committed while on U.S. Embassy property in Algiers, Algeria. We also bring many prosecutions for crimes committed in violation of Federal criminal statutes with clear extraterritorial application, such as procurement fraud. Where we can hold U.S. Government personnel and contractors accountable for crimes committed while they are working on behalf of the U.S. Government, we will do so.

III. LEGISLATIVE NEED

These successes notwithstanding, there are significant limits to our ability to prosecute sometimes egregious criminal conduct committed overseas by people working on behalf of the U.S. Government. The criminal statutes with clear extraterritorial jurisdiction make up only a subset of the Federal criminal laws, and the special maritime and territorial jurisdiction of the United States is limited. Additionally, we can only charge a violation of MEJA when we can prove that the defendant's employment "relates to supporting the mission of the Department of Defense overseas." Whether any particular defendant falls within the scope of MEJA, therefore, depends upon highly specific facts and circumstances relating to his or her employment and, in practice, this statutory language has proven difficult to apply. Cases that would otherwise be straightforward can turn into complex investigations focusing not just on the underlying criminal conduct, but also on the scope of the defendant's employment, his or her specific work duties, and other jurisdiction-related facts. These inquiries about the scope of a particular defendant's employment can be extremely challenging and resource-intensive given that they often need to be conducted in war zones or under other difficult circumstances.

Furthermore, in some instances, the relevant information concerning a defendant's employment and how it relates to the Defense Department's mission may be classified. Although the Justice Department may use procedures set out under the Classified Information Procedures Act, such procedures may not be adequate to protect national security information and also establish to a jury beyond a reasonable doubt that a defendant is subject to MEJA. In practice, this means that certain civilian U.S. Government employees and contractors can commit serious crimes overseas without fear of U.S. prosecution.

The unfortunate consequence of the current state of the law is that, for example, a Department of Defense contractor who murders a colleague in Iraq may be prosecuted under MEJA, while a contractor with another U.S. agency who commits the very same crime may not be, since he or she may not be covered by MEJA. Similarly, an employee with a non-Department of Defense agency who rapes a foreign national in the employee's diplomatic residence may be prosecuted for committing a crime within the special maritime and territorial jurisdiction of the United States, while the same person might not be able to be prosecuted if he commits the same crime in the victim's apartment.

CEJA is needed to close these gaps in the law. In the first hypothetical situation I just described, under CEJA, the Government contractor could be prosecuted for murder regardless of whether his or her employment had anything to do with the Department of Defense's mission. And in the second hypothetical situation I described, the U.S. Government employee could be prosecuted for rape regardless of where the crime occurred, and without the need for an inquiry into the precise nature of the defendant's employment.

Given the evolving nature of our engagement in various countries such as Iraq and Afghanistan, and given the large number of employees and contractors being utilized by agencies other than the Department of Defense, we view the enactment of CEJA as crucial to ensuring accountability and demonstrating to other countries that we do not give U.S. Government employees license to commit crimes overseas.

IV. Proposed Legislation

Mr. Chairman, we are pleased that you plan to introduce new legislation to close the gaps in the law. We look forward to working with your staff to make the legislation as strong as possible. In particular, to minimize potential sovereignty concerns of other countries, we hope that the legislation will preserve the authority of the relevant Chiefs of Mission and clarify that any law enforcement activities overseas related to CEJA will be conducted consistent with appropriate guidance from the Justice Department in consultation with the Department of State. It is essential that any legislation include a statutory carve-out to ensure that the legislation does not impose criminal liability on authorized intelligence activities of the United States Government. The absence of an explicit exemption for authorized intelligence activities conducted abroad would negatively impact the United States' ability to conduct such activities.

We share your goal of passing a robust and comprehensive CEJA statute that provides clear and unambiguous jurisdiction to prosecute non-Department of Defense personnel for overseas misconduct, without wasting valuable resources on unnecessary litigation and urge you to draft it in a way that focuses on the most serious, violent crimes committed abroad.

Conclusion

Since MEJA's passage in 2000, we have aggressively enforced MEJA against Department of Defense employees, contractors, and individuals accompanying them. We have also investigated a number of matters involving non-Department of Defense persons when we can establish that their employment "relates to supporting the mission of the Department of Defense overseas" or where we had extra-territorial jurisdiction under other statutes. However, under the current law, certain U.S. Government employees can commit crimes overseas without being prosecuted. The United States may not have jurisdiction and the host nation may not have the capability or willingness to prosecute. CEJA would fix this significant problem by extending U.S. jurisdiction to all non-Department of Defense employees who commit specified crimes overseas. We fully support this legislative goal, and look forward to working with the Committee as it further refines the bill.

Thank you for the opportunity to appear before you today. I would be pleased to take any questions you may have.

INDEX

A

B

C

D

E

F

G

H

I

J

K

N

O

P

Q

R

S

T

U

V

W

Y